A Place for Me in God's Tent

Terry Murphy

A Place for Me in God's Tent

Copyright © 2019 Terry Murphy
All rights reserved.
ISBN: 978-1-945976-45-2

Published by EA Books Publishing a division of
Living Parables of Central Florida, Inc. a 501c3
EABooksPublishing.com

DEDICATION

Dedicated to the one who inspired this book — the Lamb of God whose very nature and mission shines from the folds of the tabernacle. Jesus, you are awesome.

CONTENTS

ACKNOWLEDGMENTS

I want to thank the many people whose support and encouragement have been vital to finishing this project.

To Eva Marie Everson. Thank you for persevering through all the growing pains which have been part of Word Weavers International's development into a first-class writers' group. Because of your labors, I've become part of a huge writerly family whose love, help, and encouragement have been indispensable to my sanity.

To Tere, Jan, Dena, Dee, Jetta, Constance, Jeanne, Judy, and Roberta, the members of Word Weavers Page 4 and Portland East who gave me more honest and productive critiques than I can count. Thanks for reviewing many of these devotions during our meetings and for your constant coaxing to get them into print.

To my beta readers: JoAnne, Janet, Jetta, Jeanna, Barbara, Stephanie. I found it so helpful to see your varying perspectives on the tabernacle. Your suggestions have been invaluable to me as I made revisions.

To my developmental editor, Peter Lundell. Thank you for your crucial input on the final arrangement, tone, and organization of this book. Without you, it would have lost much of its impact.

To my illustrator, Debbie Smith. Thank you for reaching into heaven for your designs. I feel the touch of the Holy Spirit on your work. Readers can check out more of her work on her website: www.3-deborah-smith.pixels.com.

To the gang at EA Publishing for their valiant efforts to midwife my dream—drawing it out of my heart and delivering it into the world. Thanks especially to Cheri Cowell for repeatedly reassuring me the book was worth producing. It took a while, but your encouragement finally bore fruit.

First, last, and never least, thanks to my family for sticking with me.

Thanks to my kids and their spouses. Jeanna, James, Jared, Susmita, all four of you played a role in getting this done. Each of you gave unique suggestions which (believe it or not) I did listen to. Thanks for your gentle prodding to keep moving forward.

Charlotte, Isaac, and Maya, I can't imagine more wonderful grandchildren. You kept interrupting me with joy just when I needed it. Thank you for loving me.

Bill, thank you for so many waves goodbye and welcome-home hugs before and after all my writers conferences. Thanks for your continual encouragement throughout this journey, for remaining gracious with my mood swings and obsession with the computer toward the end, for your hugs and your friendship, and for saying yes to going ahead with the production of this book. You keep me stable. Thanks for marrying me.

Introduction

Why Are We Here?

And let them make Me a sanctuary, that I may dwell among them (Exodus 25:8).

I go to prepare a place for you. And if I go and prepare a place for you, I will come again and receive you to Myself; that where I am, there you may be also (John 14:2–3).

Scripture refers to two main dwelling places—one where God lives with human beings (first in the tabernacle, later in the temple, finally in our hearts), the other where we are destined to live with Him for all eternity. Details are light concerning what kind of place God is preparing for our future, but there's no lack of building specs for His home with us today.

In fact, because there's so much overlap between the two, if we study *God's* dwelling place, we'll automatically understand our own. The apostle Paul tells us in 1 Corinthians 6:19 that we are the temple for His Holy Spirit. If we consider the design of the earthly tabernacle, then, we'll learn a lot about how God wants our lives to merge with His.

Everything God made, including the tabernacle, is part of the grand love story He's written in creation. The main characters are Father, Son, and Holy Spirit, but we play important supporting characters in His plot line. As His narrative reveals, we are the objects of His desire.

He introduced His story with creation, explaining much of His tale in words anyone can understand. "The heavens declare the glory of God; and the firmament shows His handiwork" (Psalm 19:1). Who, after all, hasn't read a theme of rebirth and transformation in the life cycle of the butterfly? Who hasn't noted the similarity between the seasons of the earth and seasons in our lives?

The details of the tabernacle design further flesh out His story, illustrating what life with Him looks like. The design seems to shout His desire to have a tent filled with fearless children who fly into His arms and bend His ear with psalms of love and requests for help. He wants children who not only feel welcome in His tent, but make Him welcome in theirs.

This place, this habitation, was not just designed for Moses. Nor does it describe a home only for the sweet by-and-by. It's an illustration of how and where we can abide with Him in our everyday lives.

The people of Moses' day repeatedly dismantled the tabernacle for travel and reassembled it during rest periods. Each time they did, they were able to read the tabernacle's story anew. We'll do our own form of deconstruction and reconstruction as we follow the building plans in the order they were delivered to the Israelites.

The details of the tabernacle design appear three times in Scripture — when God delivered the blueprints to Moses on Mount Sinai, when Moses explained the plans to the people, and when Moses and the people finally assembled the tabernacle and began ministry in it. We'll give each of these three descriptions its own six-week part in this devotional. In Part One, we'll consider what the tabernacle design implies about us as individual dwelling places for God. In Part Two, we'll focus on what the design suggests about all believers assembling into a single tent with God in our midst. In Part Three we'll discover how Jesus Christ can be seen paralleling and fulfilling the aspects of the tabernacle.

This book is designed to be flexible. If you're short on time, simply read the devotion and prayer. If you want to see how the theme is repeated elsewhere in Scripture, move on to the "Deeper Still" segment. If you like journaling, use the opportunity to flow on with the Holy Spirit in further thoughts. If you'd rather take this journey through the tabernacle with friends, you'll find some discussion question at the end of each week's readings to help launch group conversation. Finally, make sure you check out my Facebook group for this book. Just search for "A Place for Me in God's Tent" then look for the book cover. It's a closed group to allow for a bit of privacy, but I'll let you in as soon as you request membership.

For the LORD has chosen Zion; He has desired it
for His dwelling place: "This is My resting place
forever; here I will dwell, for I have desired it"
(Psalm 132:13–14).

Prayer: As I watch You build the tabernacle, Father, show me where I come into Your story.

Part One

The Place and Me

We begin in Exodus 25, where Scripture first mentions the tabernacle. When God meets Moses on Mount Sinai, He describes exactly how to fashion His tent. In this first six-week section, we'll look at the details of the tabernacle design and consider what they say about us as individuals. What does it mean to be a dwelling place for God?

Week One

Day 1

At Home in the Wilderness

Some people love the desert. They see the stark landscape as somehow beautiful in its simplicity. I prefer landscapes that pop with color, shout with life, and ooze with moisture.

My husband and I spent several years living in New Mexico and I never got used to it. The desert sun hammers your head and its dazzling light makes your eyelids cramp from squinting. Clouds overhead float about like undelivered promises, clutching their moisture with a relentless grip. When they condescend to release it, they let it go in fits and starts. Sometimes sprinkle, sometimes deluge. Whatever they give, the relief is generally brief.

Travel through this dry place can be a mournful affair. Forsaken twigs, their bark long ago blasted white, snap underfoot. With each step, the desert invades your shoes, a teaspoon at a time.

The wilderness, in other words, is no place for sissies. It is, however, a good metaphor for life. And a good symbol for the kind of place God chooses to set up His sheltering tent. Not in a lovely garden already perfected in order and beauty. Not where life is easy or pleasant. He meets us in the midst of the chaotic desperation of our wilderness—in the center of our neediness. Ahead lies a land flowing with milk and honey to which He longs to lead us, where gardens grow and shade abounds. Until we get there, He wants to be Emmanuel—God with us in the here and now.

He's a willing companion in our journey, joining us where we are—sharing the hardship, pointing us to shelter, digging out wells of refreshment for us along the way.

In Romans 5:8, the apostle Paul says, "God demonstrates His own love toward us, in that while we were still sinners, Christ died for us." Did you get that? *While* we're still sinners, *while* we languish in our wilderness, *before* we are beautiful or perfect, He sets up His tent in the middle of our lives, hoping our thirsty souls will draw us to seek refreshment within His tent.

I will dwell among the children of Israel and will be their God. And they shall know that I am the LORD their God, who brought them up out of the land of Egypt, that I may dwell among them. I am the LORD their God
(*Exodus 29:45–46*).

Prayer: Dear God, I feel lost. I thirst for life that means something. You said You would camp where I am. Help me find You in this empty place.

Deeper Still

Take a moment to read: Isaiah 43:1–4.
Does it surprise you that God would find you so valuable? Journal your thoughts.

Day 2

A Tent is in Sight

Let's imagine ourselves as sun-weary travelers trudging through an unforgiving wilderness and consider how the tabernacle might appear to us. Our knees weary, our skin hot, our tongue and lips parched, we see a tent rise before us on the horizon like a promise.

Shelter. At last. Except, something's odd. This is not the kind of tent we expected.

The Bedouin dwellings in southern Israel are dark—almost black—as I discovered when I visited several years ago. The women marching through the desert were themselves draped from head to foot in black robes. It was counter-intuitive to my western mind. Imagining the incredible heat building up under those dark fabrics almost made my armpits sweat. I learned there was a bit of desert technology at work. The cloth indeed absorbs heat, but because hot air rises, a cooling current develops within, lifting the heat up and out.

The point is, someone living in the wilderness probably wouldn't be expecting a pale tent. They'd be looking for telltale squares of black, camelhair dwellings—tent colors that stand out against the sands and mark where salvation from the sun lies. The tabernacle, on the other hand, shimmers white on the horizon—the linen fence surrounding it fairly blends in with the pastel background.

The kingdom of God is often like that for us. It's there, but we don't see it. We think we know what we're looking for, but when we draw near, it doesn't make sense to our wilderness-oriented logic. The least of its residents are considered great. The leaders are servants. Those who expect to live here must learn how to die. The logic of the place is all wrong. Salvation is near, but it's hard to see.

In speaking of the Messiah, Isaiah 42:2 says, "He will not cry out, nor raise His voice, nor cause His voice to be heard in the street." This gleaming kingdom doesn't shout for attention either; it doesn't stand out like the dark tents against pale desert sand. It's been in sight all along—near us, even in our hearts (Romans 10:8). Now that our eyes are adjusted, let's turn aside to see this great sight. The kingdom of God used to blend in with the background of our lives, but now that we have looked for it—now that we are looking for *Him*—He promises to let us find Him.

> *You will seek Me and find Me, when you search for Me with all your heart. I will be found by you says the LORD (Jeremiah 29:13–14).*

Prayer: Almighty God, You have taken the first step and come near to me. Now help me come near to You. Now that I'm looking, help me find You.

Deeper Still

Read Jeremiah 29:11–14.
When you think of God "finding" you, does that make you nervous or excited? What difference does it make that He offers to let *you* find *Him*? Journal your thoughts.

He waits for us to be hungry enough to WANT Him - no force or pressure, but an open invitation

8

Day 3

Permission to Enter

Now that we've distinguished the tent from the background, we notice something else as we draw nearer. This is no pup tent we're approaching. It's enormous. The linen hangings surround an area somewhere around 150 feet by 75 feet, depending on how you count your cubits. Everything we could possibly need must be stocked inside. Now, if only its Resident is willing to share . . .

The one who lives in this tent has a reputation for being gracious. It is the custom of nomadic peoples to offer hospitality to strangers, but barging in without asking permission would be the height of impertinence. We'd best not presume on His welcome. As desert etiquette requires, we stand humbly, just in sight of the east-facing opening of the great tent, and wait.

Will He be as kind as some say? Will He let us come in? We look pretty mangy coming in from the desert. Will He let us track our dirt inside His clean tent? Maybe we should have washed first. Maybe we should have changed into something more presentable. Except we don't have anything more presentable and the spots on our clothes are stains that can't be scrubbed off.

We shouldn't have come. He'll never receive us. We have nothing. We are nothing.

Just as we think better of even being here, it happens. The rich tapestries part. The glorious Resident appears, approaching us with arms outstretched, His smile radiant with sincerity and joy.

He behaves as though . . . as though we are some long-lost friend, a prodigal child thought dead yet found alive. But how could that be? We know next to nothing about Him. Yet it's clear from the first moment of His greeting, He not only knows us, but sees right through us—who we are, who we were, what we've done, what we've failed to do. It's impossible, but He seems truly happy we have come.

Suddenly, what began as a journey to have our needs met has transformed into a pilgrimage to discover and be known by the remarkable Master of the tent.

The flap is open and we're invited to enter His world of abundance in the center of our world of need.

The one who comes to Me I will by no means cast out
(John 6:37).

Prayer: It seems incredible that You, the Creator of the universe, the one who holds the fate of the world in His hands, tosses stars across the horizon and calls each of them by name, would be so excited to have someone like me come near. Yet You have waited for this day since the moment I was conceived in my mother's womb. I hope You won't be disappointed You welcomed me. But here I am. Love me, Lord. And help me love You.

Deeper Still

Read John 6:35–40.
There's great certainty in the words Jesus speaks. Do they help you believe God really wants you in His tent? What reservations do you still have? Journal your thoughts.

Day 4

Into the Deep

Before we begin, read Exodus 25:10–22

You would think our Host would begin His tour with the outer, less intimate rooms of His dwelling place, at least until we get to know each other better. Instead He whisks us straight into the innermost room of the tabernacle — the Holy of Holies.

Our minds spin in disbelief. We came to the tent as dusty, weary travelers, yet here we are — privy to the most intimate domain of our Host. He's set His protocols aside for the moment as He introduces us to Himself and His tent bit by bit.

The first thing He wants us to see is the ark of the covenant. Fashioned to be one piece with its lid are two golden angelic creatures called cherubim. They face one another with their wings lifted over their heads. We suddenly remember Psalm 99:1 says the LORD dwells between the cherubim, and we realize the fiery cloud rising between these heavenly beings is God Himself filling the atmosphere around us.

We, who have never felt worthy to be here in the first place, find ourselves in the very presence of the Creator of the universe. Our knees shake and our mouth hangs open in awe. Not surprising, really. Even Moses found it difficult to stand in Exodus 40:34–35 when God's presence first took up residence in the tabernacle.

The whole scene carries remarkable similarities to a person's first encounter with the one whose life would embody many parallels to the tabernacle — the promised Messiah. A relationship with Him begins with the simple privilege of drawing near His heart and realizing we're welcome.

The awe of His majesty can be intimidating. As it was for Moses, this deep place is where the fear of the Lord becomes real. It's where we recognize with utmost clarity His absolute power, authority, and glory. All our wisdom, strength, excuses, and cleverness become insubstantial vapor. Truth fills the room and everything else collapses.

The story of His love for us begins with the golden box before us. Let's take a moment to appreciate what a privilege He's offering in showing us the depths of His heart.

The LORD is in His holy temple.
Let all the earth keep silence before Him
(Habakkuk 2:20).

Prayer: Dear Lord, what do I do now? You have overwhelmed me with Your welcome and acceptance. I stand in awe of how wonderful You are. I can only wonder how I'll ever measure up to Your standards of righteousness and perfection. I bow to Your glory. There is none like You.

Deeper Still

Read Psalm 148.

It's so fitting that all of His creation should praise Him. Which of these verses most impacts your heart? What parts of His handiwork bring you to your knees? Journal your thoughts.

Everyone, every thing, every where
offering joyful praise = the way
it should be & will be!
Attitudes of indifference, ignorance,
offense + hatred that are normal now
will be utterly removed forever! And
replaced by magnificent harmony of
voices, hearts, minds + beings united
in explosions of praise that still
won't fully express His worth!

Day 5

Wood and Gold

Before we begin, read: Exodus 25:10–11

Now that we've caught our breath from the first moment of encounter, let's take a look around.

The room housing the ark described in Exodus 25 holds special value to God. He doesn't just call it holy, He calls it His Holy of Holies. The decorating scheme is simple. Everything in the room is gold—from the walls to the ark to the cherubim above it. A fitting touch, because gold is generally used in Scripture to symbolize God's nature and righteousness.

Well, that just makes us feel about as out of place as raw lumber scattered on the floor of an opulent palace. An appropriate thought, it turns out, because wood is the scriptural symbol for humanity. How in the world can we ever fit in here? God leaves us a clue in the blueprints for the ark of the covenant.

Verses ten and eleven explain, "They shall make a chest of acacia wood. . . . And you shall overlay it with pure gold, inside and out you shall overlay it."

Because the ark is appointed to sit in the secret place of the Most High, we might expect God to require it be fashioned out of solid gold. But that would have described His heart as being filled with nothing but Himself. And life without man was never in His plan.

Just as the gold hides the wood's imperfections, just as it protects the wood from destruction by fire or rotting from moisture, just as it graces a simple wooden box with incredible value and purpose, God longs to likewise cover, protect, and endow us with significance. In a place where there's nothing but gold, in the heart of a God who is nothing but holy, we find a home, because He clothes our nakedness and ordinariness with His glory.

> *He shall cover you with His feathers, and under*
> *His wings you shall take refuge; His truth shall*
> *be your shield and buckler*
> *(Psalm 91:4).*

Prayer: Lord God, thank You for covering my weaknesses and inadequacies so I could have a home inside Your beautiful heart.

Deeper Still

Read 2 Corinthians 5:1–5.
Do you groan (or long) to be clothed and covered in the way Paul describes in this letter? How does it make you feel to know He has "prepared us for this very thing"? Journal your thoughts.

Week One

Discussion Questions

We began our journey in the desert and, once we were welcomed into the tabernacle, found ourselves swept immediately into its heart. We're only beginning to discover just how many ways God demonstrates His desire to live "up close and personal" with us. Choose one or more of the following questions to consider on your own or discuss as a group.

1. What are some of the ways God uses the tabernacle to demonstrate His desire to be part of our lives? Which of His illustrations most resonate with you?
2. It was God's idea, not ours, to set up a tabernacle right in our midst. How have you experienced God making the first move in your relationship with Him?
3. It's immediately evident the relationship God wants with us is an intimate one. What elements of your life have been most difficult to share with Him?
4. Questions? Insights? Look for "A Place for Me in God's Tent" on Facebook and join the conversation.

Week Two

Day 6

Hidden in Glory

Before we begin, read Exodus 25:12–16

I find the most remarkable aspect of the ark's wood is its utter unremarkability.

God doesn't instruct Moses to carve up a stately cedar of Lebanon for this special place. The ark (indeed the entire Holy of Holies) would be assembled from planks and pieces of ordinary *shittim* wood.

Shittim, an unimpressive, acacia-like plant, is a scruffy desert-dweller that looks more like a large bush than a tree. It's a defensive bit of herbage with long, imposing thorns that keep hungry wildlife at bay. Its dense heartwood resists both ax and carving knife.

Prickly and difficult as it is, though, the acacia contains the potential to spread its branches wide as it matures, like a thatch umbrella sheltering a sun-weary land. Entrusted to the hands of a master craftsman, this tough wood can even be fashioned and polished it into something beautiful.

I can relate to the defensive, hard-hearted acacia. I put up my thorny fists whenever I feel either man or God coming too close for comfort. And just try and dig into my inner core and attempt to work changes if you want to know how stubborn I can be—even if those changes would make me a better person. Like the humble acacia, however, when I yield to the will of my Creator, I become capable of so much more.

Even the most finely polished acacia, however, can never be transformed into a golden object worthy to rest in this holy place. The wood of the tabernacle reminds us our true loveliness and value isn't based on the great stock from which we've sprung or how mature and splendid we've become. It's a bestowed glory — one that is given and wrapped around us — which actually makes us fit to be with Him.

How appropriate then, that such ordinary wood represent mankind in the tabernacle tableau. God isn't afraid of our defensiveness or iron will. He sees to it that all our ordinariness and unloveliness, is hidden under the pure gold of His glory and holiness, making a home for the imperfect within the Perfect.

He has clothed me with the garments of salvation,
He has covered me with the robe of righteousness
(Isaiah 61:10).

Prayer: Heavenly Father, help me believe You really want me here with you. I feel so unworthy. Help me believe that when You look at me, all You see is the beauty of Christ wrapped around me, while all my imperfections are hidden from view.

Deeper Still

Read Isaiah 61:10–11.
What do you have in common with the acacia wood in the tabernacle? Can you picture yourself being covered in something so precious as gold? Isaiah speaks of being clothed and covered too. Can you believe God wants you dressed like this? Journal your thoughts.

Day 7

Fit for a Banquet

Before we begin, read: Exodus 25:23–30

From the innermost room, our Host turns our attention to a space just outside the Holy of Holies in order to describe the second piece of furniture in His tent — a table.

Not just any dining table, though. Built of acacia wrapped in gold, the table of showbread echoes the theme of Emmanuel (God with us) that the ark began. (See "Wood and Gold" on Day 5 and "Hidden in Glory" on Day 6 if you need to review.)

Here conversation deepens to communion, because any table talk will be between God and us. How striking that after the major emphasis on God's holiness and our connection to it, He points us to a symbol of conversation, family, and supply. The awesome King and Judge of the universe invites us to linger with Him the way a father might want to hang around the dinner table with his kids.

The meal on the table is measured with a dose of extravagance detailed in Leviticus 24:5–6. "Take fine flour and bake twelve loaves of bread, using two-tenths of an *ephah* a for each loaf. Set them in two rows, six in each row, on the table of pure gold before the LORD" (NIV).

Just how much bread does that make? Two-tenths of an *ephah* of flour translates to about four quarts. Four

21

quarts of flour works out to at least four and a half pounds per loaf. Add to that the weight of any liquid ingredients and you can see this is no sprinkling of breadcrumbs. With twelve of these loaves, we're talking about over fifty pounds of bread resting on the golden surface. Once more, the ordinary rubs shoulders with the extraordinary. Bread on gold. Gold on wood. Everywhere we look, God shows Himself abiding close to man.

These loaves are variously translated as the bread of the Presence, the bread of faces and the continual bread. Authorities differ on whether they were stacked or spread across the surface, but all agree these twelve loaves represented the whole family of Israel continually present before the face of God.

Stacked or laid out flat, the many loaves remind me of a wall—a wall of faces looking out from the family table toward their Father at the head. Each brick in this metaphorical wall of bread is exactly the same in size and quality, and each carries the same weight of importance. It doesn't matter whether the tribe it represents is proportionally large or small, strong or weak.

Just like the bread, whether we're rich or poor, powerful or powerless, each of us can find a continual and equally memorable resting place in His presence and before His face. Here we find the reassurance we need that He not only desires to nourish and sustain us, but to fellowship with us as a family.

See, I have inscribed you on the palms of My hands;
your walls are continually before Me
(Isaiah 49:16).

Prayer: Heavenly Father, the things that pertain to me seem insignificant compared to all that must occupy Your attention in the world. Yet You've etched a spot for me in

Your immeasurable palm and keep watch over what matters to me. Emmanuel, as You look in my direction and draw near to me, I lift my face and return Your gaze as I stumble ever closer to You.

Deeper Still

Read Psalm 145:14–21.

"The LORD is near to all." Can you picture your loaf on a level with everyone else's on God's table? What does it mean to know God is as close to you as He is to the greatest saint who ever lived? Journal your thoughts.

Day 8

Let There Be Light

Before we begin, read Exodus 25:31–40

After taking in the abundance displayed on the table, after marveling at the repeated theme of God's desire to be constantly near us, we blink a moment and realize something. We've been deep within a dark tent and yet we've been able to see everything around us. Let's turn around to see the light source across the room from the table.

The pure gold lampstand (or menorah) we're looking at resembles a tree, complete with stems, cups, calyxes, and flowers. Six branches rise from a central trunk, which forms a seventh lamp or light. It isn't made of wood covered in gold like the rest of the furniture. It's pure gold, beaten into shape by a master craftsman.

Just gold? God without man? What happened to the symbol of Emmanuel (God with us) we saw in the other pieces of tabernacle furniture? It's in the detail. God uses the language of trees—stems, branches, flowers—to describe the form of the lampstand. Once more we find God marrying wood with gold.

Six branches reach for heaven on the lampstand, but it is the seventh one—driven like a spike through their center—that holds them together and raises them high. Hammered into one piece, these seven flaming branches combine their candlepower to flood the holy place with light.

Where are we in this beautiful picture? Because human beings were created on the sixth day of creation, six is often considered as the scriptural number for mankind. Like the six side branches, we have no power of our own to raise our heads before the face of God. Not unless we are grafted into someone holy enough to stand upright in His presence and hold others up with Him.

In Isaiah 11:1 and other prophetic passages, God would promise to one day send a Savior called the "Branch." Secured to His shoulders as to the central shaft of the lampstand, we have access to the face of God. It is He who lifts our lights and helps us shine.

> *Even to your old age, I am He, and even to gray hairs I will carry you! I have made, and I will bear; even I will carry and will deliver you*
> *(Isaiah 46:4).*

Prayer: Jesus, help me cling to You. Make my attachment to You as solid as the arms of the menorah are to the central branch. Lift me up and let my light shine brightly next to Yours.

Deeper Still

Read John 15:1–8.

Jesus indicates both fruitfulness and life itself result from being securely attached to Him. Have you ever experienced a sense of uselessness or deadness when your lifestyle has carried you away from Him? Journal your thoughts.

Day 9

A Canopy of Protection

Before we begin, read: Exodus 26:1–3

After describing the lampstand, you might think God would next direct our attention to the final piece of furniture for the holy place. But He doesn't. He begins to lay out the pattern of the curtains that cover the tabernacle.

At floor level, the color scheme has been pretty much monochromatic — gold. Now we look up to see God paint with a riot of color.

Read the first verse of today's reading again. In the golden glow of the lampstand, we see angels flying over our heads. Bold threads of blue and scarlet and purple slide in and out of gleaming white linen, defining the shapes of cherubim and feathering their wings. All of this weaves a portrait of God's promise to watch over us. "He shall cover you with His feathers, and under His wings you shall take refuge. . . . For He shall give His angels charge over you, to keep you in all your ways" (Psalm 91:4, 11).

More amazing, this tapestry, when stitched and clasped together, will extend beyond what we can see. There's enough fabric to completely cover the walls (which will be described later). From inside the holy place, however, we see only a third of its beauty — the part that's directly overhead. The remainder of the curtain falls outside the golden walls. We see the cherubim above, but not those surrounding us, even though they're here.

God doesn't just cover us from above. He continues the meticulous weaving throughout the curtain, even where it will rarely be seen. Like the curtains, His protection surrounds and covers us from every angle.

Creation sends the same message. The sun is still there when the sky fills with clouds. The ground hasn't gone anywhere when snow hides it. The wind still blows though we can't feel it from inside a house. All these things testify that we see only in part.

When we can't see, when we can't feel, the tabernacle reminds us God is still here, still with us. He not only covers, but also surrounds us. Never will He leave or forsake us.

For You, O LORD, will bless the righteous;
with favor You will surround him as with a shield
(Psalm 5:12).

Prayer: Oh Father, help me believe when I can't see. Help me remember Your protection is always around me the way the curtain always surrounds the tabernacle.

Deeper Still

Read Psalm 125.
The psalmist writes of God's protection acting like a ring of mountains around us. Curtains, shields, mountains. Which picture reassures you most? Journal your thoughts.

Day 10

Loops of Great Value

Before we begin, read Exodus 26:4–6

A remarkable feature spans the angel-filled canopy above us. Clasped together at seven- or eight-inch intervals, the two halves of the linen curtain are joined with something like fancy gold and blue butterfly sutures — like a wound made whole.

The seams binding the five separate panels of each half of the grand curtain are sewn together with fine, invisible stitches. The seam directly above, however, fashioned with fifty golden clasps clinging to fifty loops, is meant to be noticed.

Elsewhere in the tabernacle, gold overlays wood. In the ceiling, gold holds fast to yarn or fabric. Once more the divine displays a connection with the earthly, the dazzling touches the humble. Like the clasps clinging to the loops, Almighty God binds Himself to us.

The humble fabric qualifies to come into contact with gold because God has endowed it with something precious which elevates its value. He has the loops drenched in blue dye.

Blue (along with purple) was likely the most expensive dye to produce in biblical times. It came from a rare and undistinguished-looking, brown and bumpy creature called *Murex trunculus* — a snail that still slides through the shallow waters of the Mediterranean today. A tiny gland beneath its shell produces snail slime, but it also contains a chemical that turns fabric blue or purple, depending on how it's processed. The snail doesn't yield its treasure easily. When its shell is smashed open to harvest the gland, the snail dies.

In other words, the loops gain their place in the tabernacle at the cost of a life.

It's easy to forget how very precious we are in God's eyes, but John 3:16 says, "God so loved the world that He gave His only begotten Son, that whoever believes in Him should not perish but have everlasting life." Sometimes it's equally hard to believe just how much He wants us to tabernacle with Him. He has spared no expense, however, to establish a place for us.

Let us give thanks to Him for His goodness and kindness, for there's none like Him in all the world.

I gave Egypt for your ransom, Ethiopia and Seba
in your place. Since you were precious in My sight,
you have been honored, and I have loved you
(Isaiah 43:3–4).

Prayer: Almighty God, who am I that You have gone to such lengths just to have me by Your side? My knees buckle at the thought of You stooping to bless me. I have become someone worth loving, but only because You have added so much to me.

Deeper Still

Read Isaiah 43:1–4.
Look how much God is willing to give for you. Do you have trouble believing you are this valuable to Him? Journal your thoughts.

Week Two

Discussion Questions

This week, we considered the significance of acacia wood in the tabernacle, our role as bread on the table, our position on the lampstand, the meaning of the great canopy overhead, and God's spare-no-expense attitude toward us. Choose one or more of the following questions to consider on your own or discuss as a group.

1. What do you have in common with acacia wood used in the tabernacle? In what ways do you think it's an appropriate symbol for humanity?
2. We considered the loaves on the table of showbread to be representative of our lives. Do you have trouble seeing yourself as measuring up equally with the other loaves on God's table? Why or why not?
3. Most of the elaborately embroidered canopy was hidden by the golden walls, yet it was still there. Can you describe a time when God proved He'd been with you all along, even though you couldn't see Him?
4. What do you think of God's willingness to go to great lengths to have you by His side?
5. Questions? Insights? Look for "A Place for Me in God's Tent" on Facebook and join the conversation.

Week Three

Day 11

The Goat Hair Tent

Before we begin, read Exodus 26:7–13

Oddly enough, as soon as God finishes describing the precious linen curtain, He starts talking about covering it up. Now, I would have understood if He had insisted on something at least as lovely as the curtains themselves for this purpose. Instead, He asks for goat hair to be woven into panels of coarse and bristly fabric.

We're talking about goat *hair*, mind you, not goat wool. The resulting tent won't be made of something soft and comfortable like the cashmere or mohair of the goat's undercoat, but of the stiff outer layer of hair that keeps the wool fluffy.

Dark. Ordinary. Familiar. This was the cloth of the common man's tent.

The linen curtain we looked at in "A Canopy of Protection" on Day 9 measured just large enough to reach over the sides of the tabernacle walls without dipping its skirts in the dust. The goat hair tent is made to spread wider, because of its eleventh panel. It hangs lower as well, because its panels are thirty cubits long to the curtains' twenty-eight. With its fabric brushing the dirt, the goat hair tent completely swallows the picture of angelic protection beneath its somber folds.

From the outside, the covered tabernacle looks much like anyone's tent. Hidden inside, though, is all that is breathtaking, light, fragrant, and priceless. Why create such artistry and cover it with something so dark and plain?

The purpose for all this tenting is to build a dwelling place for God. But He doesn't want to live there alone. To make us comfortable living with one another is going to take some doing. Adjustments will be necessary which we humans have little to no power to do anything about. God promises to send a Messiah who will make the plan possible, but He has to make Him recognizable to us, so He leaves us clues everywhere.

Some of those clues are in the tabernacle designs. When Jesus arrives, His life parallels many aspects of the tent and its ministry. The same design, however, shares some similarities to our heart when it becomes a dwelling place for God.

When we open our tent flaps and welcome Christ to take up residence, we still look as ordinary as the goat hair curtains on the outside. From the inside, however, everything looks different. His ever-glowing lampstand radiates with hope. His heavy-laden table continually sustains.

We can be hard-pressed, perplexed, persecuted, or struck down on the outside, but the presence of God in our hearts keeps us from being crushed, sunken in despair, or destroyed on the inside (2 Corinthians 4:7–16). When we look up from within this secret place, we aren't greeted with the dark folds of goat hair visible to everyone else. We gaze on the beauty and power of His heavenly linen curtains draped over us.

If your "goat hair tent" has been feeling dark and empty, Jesus longs to take up residence within you. He'll bring the light, set the table, and bring the glory with Him as He spreads His beautiful canopy over you. Open your heart and let Him hear your words of welcome.

Behold, I stand at the door and knock. If anyone hears My voice and opens the door, I will come in to him and dine with him, and he with Me
(Revelation 3:20).

Prayer: Jesus, I need light and hope. I'm afraid of what You might think when You see the state my tent is in, but I'm asking You to come near anyway and share Your life with me.

Deeper Still

Read Song of Solomon 4:1–10.
Do you have trouble imagining God speaking to you with such passion? What makes it so hard to believe? Journal your thoughts.

Day 12

Skins and Leather

Before we begin, read Exodus 26:14

We come to an odd place in our tour of the tabernacle. "You shall also make a covering of ram skins dyed red for the tent, and a covering of badger skins above that."

That's it. One verse to describe the final two coverings. After all the detailed descriptions for the curtains, tent, and furniture, these layers almost seem like an afterthought. No measurements. No quantities. No stitching together. No indication whether they completely envelope the tabernacle or simply rest on its roof like a double toupee.

The first of these layers has the tiniest bit of description. The ram skins are dyed red. Dying animal hides requires they be tanned—a putrid affair involving scraping off hair and soaking the skins in vats of chemicals such as lime, vinegar, fermenting bran and . . . hold your nose . . . urine or dung. You get the picture (or rather the stench).

No wonder tanners, their arms and legs permanently discolored from sloshing around in those vats and their clothing hopelessly infused with the perfume of excrement, were relegated to live and work on the outskirts of town. The leather of the tabernacle suffers a similar indignity. After all the distress of dying, the reddened covering is hidden under the badger skins where no one can see it, either inside the tent or out.

Can you relate? After soaking in the harsh vat of suffering, have you felt smeared and bloodied with the stench and stain of life? The lingering shame and sorrow of these experiences can leave us on the emotional outskirts of life—separated, often, from even the closest of friends.

There's mercy in hiding the red-stained leather, however. God covers it with a layer of warm, protective, untanned skins.

Life has a habit of "tanning" us with episodes of hardship and sacrifice. Though these seasons of suffering seem to hurt beyond measure, God is well aware. He takes account of our red-leather times and places a permanent remembrance of them in His tabernacle.

He knows the cost of dying our "ram skins." Taking on flesh, Jesus made Himself intimately familiar with being a human under pressure, a person in pain. He has tasted the sorrow of being held in low esteem, of being cast off, and rejected.

Over us He drapes a protective covering of love—soft and warm as a badger skin—forming a hiding place for our hearts and a refuge from the storms.

> *The LORD also will be a refuge for the oppressed,*
> *a refuge in times of trouble. And those who know*
> *Your name will put their trust in You; for You,*
> *LORD, have not forsaken those who seek You*
> *(Psalm 9:9–10).*

Prayer: Some days life is just too much to bear, Jesus. Hide me under Your badger skin of love and wrap me in the warmth of Your protection.

Deeper Still

Read Psalm 46.

The psalm describes many ways God acts as our refuge —
through faithfulness, strength, and peace. Which of these
verses most comforts you when you think of God
surrounding you? Journal your thoughts.

Day 13

Do You See What I See?

Before we begin, read Exodus 26:15–30

With the weight of all this fabric and leather and skin, it's not surprising the tabernacle needs a sturdy support to keep it from collapsing.

And what a support system! Once more, God calls for tough acacia wood — this time, hewn into planks, covered in gold, and set upright in heavy silver sockets buried in the earth. No nails mar the precious metal coating. Instead, each series of upright boards is decked out with golden rings. Long poles of gold-covered acacia thread their way through the rings, locking each set of boards into a distinct wall. Where two walls meet, more gold rings slip over the heads of the end planks, stabilizing and unifying the tabernacle, board to board, and wall to wall.

Supported on this firm structure, the linen curtains, goatskin tent, red ram skins, and furry pelts find a secure and un-collapsible resting place. Ordinary poles may suffice for other tents, but this one requires walls — walls of gold with silver baseboards to reflect the glory of the furniture, to magnify the glow of the lamplight, to lift the beautiful canopy ten cubits (roughly fifteen feet) overhead. These walls shout strength and majesty and security.

The higher the walls tower above us, however, the smaller we feel. The more the gold and silver shine, the more we notice how poor our reflected image looks bouncing back at us. Wherever we turn, whatever we look at, we see our own faces, making us more conscious than ever of how far short we fall compared to this glory. The walls are strong. We are weak. The canopy is exalted. We are low. The gold and silver are pure. We are not. We wish we could hide, be invisible, but He will not allow it. We are forced to look at ourselves.

As uncomfortable as this makes us, it helps us realize the adjustments needed in our lives and how weak we are in the face of making the changes. Some alteration will be necessary to make us feel more at home here. But who is equal to the task of making the upgrade?

Now is a good time to remember that we're here by invitation. The one who welcomed us into the tabernacle sees everything we see in these reflections. Perhaps He wants us to realize that, though we are small, He sees us. Though we are weak, our form is ever before His face. All the strength, all the beauty of this place, is built not just to impress us with who He is, but to house us, to wrap around us, to protect us, to hold us.

Listen to Him whisper. "You aren't here because you are worthy. You're not here because you're great. You're here because I love you and want you with Me forever. We both see those things that make you feel out of place. Don't worry. I have a plan."

The LORD did not set His love on you nor choose you because you were more in number than any other people. . . .
but because the LORD loves you
(Deuteronomy 7:7–8).

Prayer: Father God, I'm overwhelmed with the difference between Your glory and my non-glory. Lead me through the upgrade I need while I remind myself I'm here by invitation.

Deeper Still

Read Psalm 139.
Does it make you uncomfortable to realize how well God knows you, or does it reassure you? What do you think He has in mind for your upgrade? Journal your thoughts.

Day 14

Where Heaven and Earth Meet

Let's take a moment to put what we've learned into perspective.

Imagine standing at the eastern end of the holy place and looking in. If we stretch out our arms, we can't touch the north or south walls because they're fifteen feet apart. At the far western end, down a forty-five-foot corridor of gold paneling, rises the third wall. Just in front of it, angelic sentinels kneel atop the glorious ark of the covenant.

Above our head floats the linen ceiling, awash with soaring cherubim. To our right, a golden table, heavy with bread, sends us the aroma of fresh loaves and the fragrance of frankincense. To our left, the enormous lampstand fills our eyes with light and our lungs with the smell of burning olive oil. Together they trigger a sense of hunger and an expectation of satisfaction.

Any disturbances outside the tent are muffled by the layers of fabric, leather, and wood. Distractions of everyday life are hidden from view. We are alone with the Master of the tent.

This is the kingdom of God—a place in our hearts where peace isn't governed by what's going on outside. It's the tabernacle nestled within, the Tent of Meeting where we can rest a minute and be alone with God, find restoration, and renew our strength.

Just as we're about to lose ourselves in wonder, we feel the sand of the desert tickle our toes and the rocks of the wilderness pumice our heels. Despite its elaborate decorations and materials, there is no floor in the tabernacle. No carpet separates our feet from the ground. The contrast between the beauty soothing our eyes and the roughness irritating our soles is unsettling.

This is, as Henry Soltau puts it in *The Tabernacle: the Priesthood and the Offerings*, the "anomalous connection of beauty and barrenness; of preciousness and worthlessness; the incorruptible with the perishable. . . . The heavens have been opened over our head. We worship and hold converse with God in the highest glory. And yet our members are here upon this earth." (Soltau 1972, 111)

It's hard to look at what *should* be while still being painfully aware of what *is*. This, however, is the very place we must remember the earth and the needs around us. Feet that grind against the sand remind us to make earthly requests during our time of worship.

Here, where heaven and earth meet, is where faith is born — where we come to believe that all things really are possible, even on earth. We stand at the headwaters of the River of Life. It bubbles up from within us and pours out our mouths. "Thy kingdom come, Thy will be done on earth as it is in Heaven."

In everything by prayer and supplication, with thanksgiving, let your requests be made known to God (Philippians 4:6).

Prayer: Father, here am I in Your tabernacle — experiencing heaven, but feeling the earth. Show me how to pray, so Your Kingdom reigns over the requests I bring You today.

Deeper Still

Read Luke 11:1–13.

Have you ever felt guilty spending so much of your prayer time bringing your earthly needs to the Lord? What percentage of Jesus' prayer had to do with earth? What do you think that means about God's tolerance to hear our requests? Journal your thoughts.

Day 15

Blended Threads

Before we begin, read Exodus 26:31–33

Before our Host shows us the final piece of furniture inhabiting the holy place, He introduces us to the impressive doorway hanging between this room and the Holy of Holies — the veil.

Woven of the same material and pattern as the curtain, the veil almost looks like a portion of the ceiling has dropped between us and the ark.

And it's massive. At fifteen feet tall and just as wide, the veil is imposing in size and strength. Its cherubim loom over us the way we imagine the angels would have guarded the way to the garden of Eden. It all makes us take a step back.

Even the thread colors intimidate us. Like the blue and purple dyes we learned about in "Loops of Great Value" on Day 10, the scarlet color is produced by crushing. This time it's a type of scale insect that gets smashed. Initially, all we can focus on is the cost, the cost, the cost of what's before us.

Jesus will likewise ask us to face some costly prospects in the New Testament. There will be crosses to take up and tribulations to endure if we choose to follow Him. Like contemplating the veil, the possibilities can make us anxious. "Can I pay this price? Can I drink this cup?" Former ways may suffer demolition. Persecution and hardship are sure to come. How can we hope to finish the type of race the veil seems to promise?

Hebrews 12:1–2 says Jesus endured His race "for the joy that was set before Him." Where is the joy in the veil design?

Where gold touches wood in the tabernacle, we see God covering and protecting man. In the veil, the blue of the heavens lies next to the scarlet of human blood. Combined, they draw heaven and earth together in a new and wonderful way. Where they meet, a new color appears between the holy blue and the human red — purple, the color of royalty.

When we join our lives to God, we too take on a new tone. God confers us with a royal authority that enables us to come boldly into the tabernacle. On behalf of others, we ask whatsoever we will and believe He will hear. We dare to grasp heaven and pray it into the earth. Though life in the tabernacle means sharing in the crushing promised by the veil, it also means sharing in the joy of becoming like Him and using His authority to overcome tribulations.

The gold panels in the tabernacle may reflect us as we are, but the blended threads of the veil picture us as we can be, when we fully entwine our lives with His.

It has not yet been revealed what we shall be,
but we know that when He is revealed, we shall
be like Him, for we shall see Him as He is
(1 John 3:2).

Prayer: Lord Jesus, help me blend smoothly with You in thought, word and deed.

Deeper Still

Read 1 Peter 4:12–14.

Peter tells us sharing Christ's suffering means sharing His joy as well. How does knowing this help you endure hardships? Journal your thoughts.

Week Three

Discussion Questions

This week, we considered what the goat hair curtains, and the skins the leather covers, have to say about our challenges in life. Between the glimpse of our own reflections in the gold walls and the feel of dirt between our toes, we grasped the importance of praying heaven into earth. Finally, we stood before the veil and marveled at the honor of being in His sanctuary. Choose one or more of the following questions to consider on your own or discuss as a group.

1. Review the characteristics of the goat hair curtains. Which of these elements best expresses how you see yourself?
2. Can you describe a time you felt like you were being "tanned" like the red leather? Looking back, did the Lord provide a "badger skin" hiding place for you either during or after the tanning process?
3. The dirt floor of the tabernacle reminds us we're residents of two separate worlds. What kind of situations make this dual citizenship feel most awkward for you? How do you reconcile the two?
4. Questions? Insights? Look for "A Place for Me in God's Tent" on Facebook and join the conversation.

Week Four

Day 16

The Woven Door

Before we begin, read Exodus 26:36–37

Last time, we faced west to contemplate the veil separating us from the Holy of Holies. Today, our Host spins us 180 degrees to consider "the door" dropping over the eastern entrance to the holy place.

Fashioned of the same materials and colors as the veil, this screen is "made by a weaver." No cherubim grace this drapery. Instead, Henry W. Soltau suggests the pattern is a simple weaving in and out of the differently colored threads. (Soltau 1972, 69)

I can't say for certain, but I expect the linen threads form the "warp" of the fabric—its white fibers running lengthwise on the loom. To blend the other colors in, weavers lift alternating rows of the warp, then thread the blue or scarlet or purple "weft" fibers back and forth across its width.

From a distance, our eyes see the colors merge into something of a solid purple. If we step closer, we can see the looping colors making a tiny pattern. Like pixels of color, little squares run across the surface in a violet tweed.

Let's lean over the weaver's shoulder and watch the colors rise and fall against each other on the loom. Red rises, then dips under the white. Blue bends downward and white climbs over it. Purple threads twist away, then return to sight. Through it all, the white linen warp maintains its contact with every color in the weft, while directing the whole pattern forward. Blue, purple, red, white. A bit repetitive perhaps, but the end result is a beautiful consistency.

Life tends to run in cycles as well. One moment our hearts soar with the heavenly blue of a "mountain top" experience, the next they descend back to everyday living. One situation needs a bold, authoritative response to rise and meet it. The next one requires quietness and trust to rule. Other times, only the scarlet thread of sacrifice will bring us victory.

Sometimes it feels like a weaver's shuttle is constantly rushing back and forth across our loom—bustling with motion, but thread-thin in forward progress. This tedious twisting and rising and falling, however, weaves strength of character into the fabric of our being. We learn consistency and patience, gain practice in both active faith and quiet expectation. We learn by experience that Paul was right when he wrote Philippians 4:13. We really can do all things through Christ who strengthens us.

Meanwhile, God is so proud of what He's fabricating in us, that He displays the purple proof of our destiny as kings and priests at the door of His tabernacle, where any passer-by can see it.

As we rise and fall through life's cycles then, let's not grow weary. May we grip His righteous hand as tightly as weft clings to warp. The straight threads of Christ's perfection will carry us steadily forward, even when it doesn't feel like we're moving at all.

*Everywhere and in all things I have learned both
to be full and to be hungry, both to abound and to
suffer need. I can do all things through Christ who
strengthens me
(Philippians 4:12–13).*

Prayer: Keep me steady on Your loom, Lord Jesus, as this situation cycles through to the next. Help me remember You're moving me forward even when it feels like I'm standing still.

Deeper Still

Read Romans 5:1–5.
"Hope does not disappoint." How does that line help you get through the ups and downs of life? Journal your thoughts.

Day 17

Feeling The Heat

Before we begin, read Exodus 27:1–8

Outside the tent, there is only one piece of furniture made of acacia, and its overlay is bronze instead of gold. Bronze might protect the altar's interior from being consumed in flames, but it can't protect it from the heat.

Guilt requires our attention — it filters through our conscience the way the heat of the altar penetrates bronze. The discomfort compels us to seek relief, and we are good at finding ways to do that.

We try claiming innocence. "This law isn't fair. It doesn't apply to me." Better yet, we decide it was created by societal pressures not some all-powerful God. No matter how we try and justify ourselves, however, our sense of guilt keeps smoldering.

Ever try and shift the blame? "They made me do it," I say so I grab a burning coal from my own altar and light fire to someone else's. It doesn't matter how much blame I heap on others, my own guilt keeps burning. Though we try and snuff guilt's flame by ignoring it, it's like a forest fire gone underground — some careless kick of dirt can easily rekindle the blaze.

God protects me from the full penalty of sin the way bronze wraps around wood, but still allows the heat of my guilt to come through. If I can't *feel* that guilt, I won't feel sorrow for what I've done wrong. Without sorrow, I cannot fully repent. Without repentance, the sacrifice on the altar still burns for me, but it burns in vain.

Guilt isn't meant to be our permanent companion. Its heat should move us to what Paul wrote about in 2 Corinthians 7:10, a Godly sorrow that leads to repentance without regret. Once that happens, our sin goes up in smoke with the sacrifice and we walk away cleansed and forgiven.

If we're feeling the burn, let's skip the avoidance responses and head straight to our knees in confession. As we do, God will be standing ready at His altar with a Sacrifice who is just dying to take our place in the fire.

He who covers his sins will not prosper, but
whoever confesses and forsakes them will have mercy
(Proverbs 28:13).

Prayer: Father, I do not like feeling guilty. Help me stand still and face it anyway. Let me walk straight to You and admit my faults, so You can wash me white as snow again.

Deeper Still

Read Psalm 51:1–13.
Is there something burning a hole in your conscience? As you make an honest confession to the Lord, picture Jesus taking it to the brazen altar and sending it up in smoke. Journal your thoughts.

Day 18

The Fence of Grace

Before we begin, read Exodus 27:9–15

The courtyard fence separates us from the world, but it also surrounds us with something that enables us to rest in the presence of God even when we don't feel as righteous as the white linen around us.

Let's look at the math of all this linen to see if we can determine what the fence is trying to say to us.

The courtyard is laid out like a giant rectangle. Measured in cubits, it is one hundred by fifty. Twenty pillars dot the north and south sides, while ten stand at both the east and west ends. That means a total of three hundred cubits of linen circle the perimeter on sixty evenly spaced pillars. The posts act as frames, highlighting five-cubit squares of linen all the way around the courtyard — sixty squares in all.

All these numbers (300, 100, 60, 50, 20, 5) have something in common: they're all divisible by five. What should we think of when we see all these fives in the courtyard?

This number often appears in Scripture connected to something of the miraculous. In Leviticus 25, for example, God announces there will be a Year of Jubilee every fifty years — a time when debt is wiped out and slaves go free. In 1 Samuel 17, David picks up five smooth stones from the river to defeat Goliath. In Luke 9, Jesus tells a crowd of five thousand to sit down in groups of fifty before feeding them with five loaves and a couple fish. On top of that, we carry our personal fives—five senses and five digits on each hand with which to engage and understand our world. These are gifts, given by the grace of our Creator, which benefit our lives and aid us in our journey.

Perhaps for some of these reasons, five has become known as the number of grace—undeserved favor God sends our way, even if that means dispatching the miraculous on our behalf.

Stand in the courtyard and spin around. Can you see it? Can you hear it in the five-by-five squares around the yard? "Grace!" they repeat sixty times around the fence. Virtually all the measurements surrounding us in the courtyard cry out to us in their factors of five, "Grace, grace. Multiplied grace!"

Consider where the Architect who drew the tabernacle blueprints lines up this message of comfort. Not in the deep and quiet Holy of Holies, but around the courtyard—the noisy, bustling, crowded, bloody, outskirts of the tabernacle.

Have you been there? Where crowds jostle and send you spinning, where dung hides in wait for your next footstep, where you can't hear yourself think, but you're painfully aware of the wailing prayer requests of others in the tent.

Away from the peaceful center, away from the comforting presence of God where we often find ourselves, the courtyard fence proclaims God's love and care for us in its every measurement. In the very place we feel far from Him, He wraps His curtains around us. Enfolding us in grace, yearning to clothe and encircle us with His every benefit.

God's favor, His merciful behavior toward us, His compassion and acceptance, form the walls of the house we live in with Him. Walls that separate us for His purposes. Walls that withstand. Walls that enclose us with protection, goodness, and comfort. Inside, we are accepted, beloved, and secure.

For by grace you have been saved through faith,
and that not of yourselves; it is the gift of God
(Ephesians 2:8).

Prayer: Oh Father, I'm so grateful to be hemmed in by Your grace and acceptance. Regardless of my failures, You love me still. Confident in Your confidence, Lord, enable me to run this marathon of life in a way that will make You proud.

Deeper Still

Read Ephesians 2:13–18.
Paul writes about the "far off" and the "near." Which one are you today? Can you hear Jesus' message of peace to you either way? Journal your thoughts.

Day 19

The Courtyard Gate

Before we begin, read Exodus 27:12–16

If we go outside the courtyard and take a walk around its perimeter, we see nothing but pristine white along three sides of the fence. The north, west, and south walls are dressed with single lengths of fabric (about 150 feet's worth for the north and south sides, and 75 for the west).

Revelation 19:8 makes a connection between linen and righteousness, so the perfection of all this fabric seems to make it a wall of exclusion. Does the way inside require we match it with perfect character?

In the New Testament, Jesus seems to indicate we do. In Matthew 5:20 He says, "Unless your righteousness exceeds the righteousness of the scribes and Pharisees, you will by no means enter the kingdom of heaven." Scribes and Pharisees were sticklers for following the law in all its detail. Can you imagine *exceeding* that?

The apostle Paul would eventually claim we have all sinned and fallen short of the glory of God (Romans 3:23). How, then, shall we imperfect humans cross this fence of perfection to gain access to the loving God inside?

Just in time, our Host brings us to the fourth and eastern wall of the courtyard. This part of the fence isn't fabricated from a single swath of cloth. It's made of three separate panels. Each of the two side panels are made of white linen. The center panel, though, has color dancing across its thirty-five-foot span in familiar threads of blue and purple and scarlet.

For the third time—first in the veil for the Holy of Holies, then in the screen for the holy place, and now in the gate of the courtyard—these three colors mark a clear and distinctive way in. Once more, the blue of heaven touches the red of earth to set off the stately purple of royalty, as we saw in "Blended Threads" on Day 15.

Jesus says the gateway to life is narrow and difficult to enter in Matthew 7:13–14, but He doesn't say it's inaccessible. The gateway into the courtyard is narrow compared to the three-hundred-cubit perimeter, but when we see how many people it is fashioned to accommodate, it becomes surprisingly wide.

The fence of the courtyard leads us directly to this gate—the single legitimate way into God's presence that is somehow related to the colors on its surface.

With His heavenly character as the Son of God, His earthly nature as the Son of Man, and His sinless state of righteousness, Jesus perfectly exemplifies the threads and linen of the courtyard gate. In John 10:7–10, He even calls Himself the "door" of the sheepfold. In John 14:6 He says He's the "way" to the Father.

If we take His hand, He'll take us where we can otherwise not go. His own perfection has made a way through the pristine fence. There's no need to try struggling measuring up to the righteousness of the Pharisees. Jesus is the open gate. Through Him, everyone is welcome at God's front door.

Jesus said to him, "I am the way, the truth, and the life.
No one comes to the Father except through Me"
(John 14:6).

Prayer: Lord God, every other way to You is blocked by imposing walls of perfection. Help me find the beautiful gate You have fashioned in Jesus—a gate left open just for me.

Deeper Still

Read John 10:1–10.

Did you notice the sheep don't go through the door without an escort? How does it help you to know you aren't alone as you hunt for the entrance to God's heart? Journal your thoughts.

Day 20

Fit for the Tabernacle

Before we begin, read Exodus 28:1–8

God describes the wardrobe He wants his high priest Aaron to wear as consisting of six pieces—a breastplate, an ephod (or vest), a robe, a tunic, a turban, and a sash.

He manages to fill almost an entire chapter listing His requirements for the elaborate ephod and the breastplate to be attached to it. The vest-like ephod is woven from the same type of materials we found in the courtyard gate, the screen for the holy place, the veil, and the ceiling of the Holy of Holies. The familiar blue, purple and scarlet threads in Aaron's vest, however, come with an extra splash we haven't seen in the other linen materials—gold threads.

Imagine the craftsmanship required to pound gold thinly enough to use as thread without getting it so fine it disintegrates in the process. This thin filament has to be worked in and out of the other threads without breaking.

Can't you just see Aaron, once he gets to put the ephod over the tunic and approach the Holy of Holies? His chest looks much like the veil before him, except it has an extra bling of gold shimmering from it. Gold decorates other articles of his wardrobe as he enters the quiet room—chains and rings of gold bind the gem-encrusted breastplate to the ephod, and golden bells tinkle brightly against the pomegranates of yarn at the hem of his robe. Still more gold glimmers from a crown attached to his turban.

Do you remember how gold covered and glorified the humble acacia wood of the furniture? Here in the golden threads of the ephod, the mark of the Creator weaves throughout the garments of an otherwise common human being. God's life is fused with man's in a new and wonderful way. He decorates us with the same colors and splendor He used to decorate the tabernacle we're assigned to maintain.

When we first arrived in the tabernacle, the gold plating on the walls and furniture comforted us with the knowledge of God's desire to cover and protect us. Now we see Him replace our insufficient clothing, as He weaves His own nature in and out of ours. The more we allow Him to clothe us, the more beauty and value He provides us. His garments help us feel more fit to walk in and out among His Holy rooms.

For as many of you as were baptized into
Christ have put on Christ
(Galatians 3:27).

Prayer: Lord Jesus, weave Yourself into every facet of my life. Let the glory of who You are sparkle from me so that others know it's You who makes me beautiful.

Deeper Still

Read Colossians 3:8–17.
Paul recommends a lot of taking off and putting on in these verses — exchanging parts of our human nature for parts of Christ's Godly nature. Which of these exchanges are most difficult for you? Journal your thoughts.

Week Four

Discussion Questions

This week, we studied what the door to the holy place, the heat of the brazen altar, and the courtyard fence have to say about concepts such as guilt, grace, and the importance of keeping steady. We found the true gate into God's dwelling place and had our first introduction to the priestly garments. Choose one or more of the following questions to consider on your own or discuss as a group.

1. Have you felt yourself cycling through situations like the threads on the loom did as the tabernacle door was being woven? How has God kept you steady in the face of change?
2. What's your first reaction to guilt? Denial? Justification? Avoidance? How can you encourage yourself to just go ahead and admit your sin?
3. Can you describe an experience where you felt "hemmed in by grace" in the midst of a chaotic circumstance? How did it comfort and encourage you in your trial?
4. The gold lamination of the tabernacle furniture was a promise of divine protection, while the gold in the priestly garments pointed to divinely ordained dignity. Which of these is the most difficult for you to accept from the Lord and why?

5. Questions? Insights? Look for "A Place for Me in God's Tent" on Facebook and join the conversation.

Week Five

Day 21

Unexpected Access

Before we begin, read Exodus 28:9–30

The only one God allows to wear the beautiful costume we're examining is Aaron. Once he dies, only one of his sons will put it on after him, then one of his grandsons, and so on down the line. Although the honor of wearing this garment is reserved for the high priest, and he alone sets foot in the Holy of Holies, God uses a bunch of stones to bring the entire family into the tabernacle with him.

Two onyx stones will perch on Aaron's shoulders, with six names etched in beautiful calligraphy on each one. Rueben, Judah, Issachar, Benjamin. . . . One by one, twelve patriarchal names appear on the gems. They aren't carved in onyx to memorialize these lone individuals, but the entire tribe belonging to each one. Tribes are made up of clans. Clans consist of families. Families are filled with many members. Individuals come into families through birth, adoption, or marriage. No matter how their membership was achieved, every descendent is represented by his or her patriarch's name on the onyx stone.

On Aaron's shoulders, all tribes rank equally. They appear on a level with every other tribe and share the same beauty of the onyx.

Meanwhile, another group of stones carrying the same twelve names rides into the tabernacle on the high priest's breastplate. Each is etched onto its own particular type of gem and set in gold. Aaron wears this part of his vestment strapped tightly over his heart. Unlike the onyx stones, each of these gems holds a distinctive position on the high priest's breast and shows off each tribe in a unique way.

When we enter God's presence, we come in like these stones—equal on the shoulders of the promised Messiah, yet each with our particular beauty and station on His breast.

When Jesus enters the holy place in the heavenly tabernacle and stands before God as His Great High Priest, the Father sees more than twelve names. He sees millions. Whoever we are—old, young, rich, poor, male, female—we have a continual dwelling place deep in the tabernacle as living stones.

Whether we feel like a common rock or a beautiful gem, God knows us intimately and loves us equally. "See," He says in Isaiah 49:16, "I have inscribed you on the palms of My hands; your walls are continually before Me."

> *"They shall be Mine," says the LORD of hosts, "on the day that I make them My jewels. And I will spare them as a man spares his own son who serves him"*
> *(Malachi 3:17).*

Prayer: What comfort it brings me, Jesus, to know that You continually present my name before the Father. Help me remember just how close You are and how important my welfare is to You, so I can learn to trust Your loving kindness no matter what may come.

Deeper Still

Read Isaiah 49:13–19.
When trials come, how does knowing God never forgets you change your outlook? Journal your thoughts.

Day 22

A Step of New Beginnings

Before we begin, read Exodus 29:1–9

We'll look more deeply at the priestly garments later. For now, let's discover how our Host wants to prepare His ministers for duty.

They're to begin with a process called "hallowing," which sets a person or thing apart for a particular function. In this case, the priests would be separated from worldly roles to minister exclusively to the Lord.

Why should we care about how Old Testament priests prepare for duty? Are any of us connected to the tribe of Levi and authorized to serve in the capacity Aaron and his sons did?

It turns out God has always dreamed about having a family made entirely of priests. As soon as He got His people out of Egypt, God told them in Exodus 19:6 they were destined to become "a kingdom of priests and a holy nation." It's a dream He still holds for His family today.

You may not have had such high aspirations when you first entered His tent. Personally, I just wanted a refuge from the wilderness, a hiding place from life's difficulties, a heavenly Father with answers. God, however, loves dreaming big—especially when it comes to His children.

The first step God describes in the hallowing process is taking a bath. Verse 4 of today's reading says, "Aaron and his sons you shall bring to the door of the tabernacle of meeting, and you shall wash them with water."

There doesn't seem to be anything fancy about their bath. No soap. No scrubbing. A quick dunk in the rinse cycle and they are done.

Water. A simple substance with dual potential. As a flood, it can drown. As a fountain, it revives. The priests' bath is reminiscent of the Israelites walking from slavery to freedom between the waves of the Red Sea and similar to the penitents rising from death to life in the New Testament baptism of John. The visit to the laver is like an initiation, an opening move in a complicated dance.

Our dip in God's pool is the first celebration of our tabernacle lives. It's a bit like taking the first step of marriage by having a wedding ceremony. Many lessons will follow as we learn to live with our new spouse, but this is the one that sweeps us up and carries us across the threshold into a new way of life.

When we come to the tent asking for refuge, we are each invited into the bath we call baptism. At a wedding, a minister may ask whether we take this step of our own free will. In the tabernacle, God asks whether life with Him is what we freely choose.

As a gesture of agreement—our physical "I do"—we allow the waters to flow over us. In a moment, we are delivered from our old, limited life to begin a new and abundant one. The heat of the wilderness washes away, our skin cools and we are refreshed. Jesus calls this moment being born again.

Our High Priest Jesus took His bath in Matthew 3:13–17. Let us take a deep breath and follow Him into waters destined for priests. Who knows where this first step may lead?

Let us draw near with a true heart in full assurance of faith, having our hearts sprinkled from an evil conscience and our bodies washed with pure water (Hebrews 10:22).

Prayer: Heavenly Father, at Your invitation I take a step of faith into Your bath. I choose a life with You in Your tabernacle. Let the old wash away and this new life begin!

Deeper Still

Read Titus 3:3–7.

These verses speak of regeneration and renewal being connected with this water bath. What needs renewal in your life? What would "starting over" look like for you? Journal your thoughts.

Day 23

Grabbing a Strong Bull

Before we begin, read Exodus 29:10–11

After Aaron and his sons wash and dress, God tells Moses to have them haul a bull to the altar. Not a cow, mind you, not even a good-sized steer, but a hulking mound of snorting, pawing-the-ground muscle. If you've ever gazed across a field of grazing bovines, you won't have trouble distinguishing which is the bull among them.

What are they to do with the beast? Bring it before the tabernacle of meeting and put their hands on its head. I wonder just how easy they'd find it to bring a mass of living power forward like that without losing control. Can you imagine them getting the monster to the door of the tent, then pressing in to lay hands on his head? I'm guessing this might initiate some dampening armpits.

Bulls aren't known for their gentle nature. It takes courage to grab one by the nose ring or horns. But to box him in and grope for his head? How well would a bull tolerate this kind of treatment?

Perhaps that's what makes the bull appropriate as the sin offering. Most of us would no more agitate a sin in our heart than disturb a bull in a field.

Better to ignore sin than wrangle it to a place where we have to deal with it. Better to avoid touching it than risk retribution from horns and hooves on the way to repentance. Unfortunately, sin is much like a bull left loose in a field—it's only going to breed more problems if we leave it alone.

The first step in subduing sin is to call it what it is, to recognize its power, to admit it won't be tamed. Frightening and dangerous as it may be, we must identify our strong and willful sins, reach out our hands, and drag them to the tabernacle door. If we commit to bringing the strong bull of our willfulness-on-testosterone to the Lord, He will oversee its destruction.

We each have issues in our lives we'd rather leave alone—things we'd rather not recognize as wild bulls. Nevertheless, we know they're unsettling our hearts. Let us take a chance that God's way really will calm what disquiets us. Let us dare to snatch those things we know are wrong in our lives and bring them into the tabernacle. The Lord will lay the beast low for us and set us free.

If we say that we have no sin, we deceive ourselves,
and the truth is not in us. If we confess our sins,
He is faithful and just to forgive us our sins and to
cleanse us from all unrighteousness
(1 John 1:8–9).

Prayer: Father God, help me. My will snorts like a bull. Give my heart courage to seize the truth by the nose and bring it to You.

Deeper Still

Read Psalm 32.
David's emotions change from "groaning" to great rejoicing when he finally breaks his silence about his sin in this psalm. Think about your before-and-after feelings

when you finally admitted your faults to the Lord.
Journal your thoughts.

Day 24

Slaying the Beast

Before we begin, read Exodus 29:10–14 again

When all these priests reach for an arguably skittish bull at the tabernacle door, we might assume a quick touch would count as "laying on of hands." Surely more than that would be excessively dangerous. But in *The Tabernacle, the Priesthood, and the Offerings*, Henry W. Soltau suggests the word used for "putting" their hands on the bull's head actually implies leaning heavily against it. (Soltau 1972, 363)

This firm contact is necessary because, in some mysterious way, God causes their sin to entirely transfer to the bull in the process.

Though the bull is labeled as the "sin offering" in English, the word "offering" doesn't even appear in the Hebrew. The priests' sacrifice for the hallowing ceremony is called *chattaah*, meaning "sinful thing" or simply "sin." In other words, as the priests press their hands upon his head, the bull will not only *take on* their sin, he will *become* the sinful thing itself.

Another reason the we need to lean on the "bull" of our sin might be to make sure we feel it, smell it, fear its power. Lightweight apologies like, "Lord, *if* I have offended You in any way . . . " are simply insufficient. They cost us little and mean less.

Leaning on the bull means getting specific, acknowledging our sins by name. In the process, we'll catch a whiff of what they really smell like to God, feel the rippling strength of their muscles beneath the skin of our bad habits, tremble at the realization of where our choices have brought us.

As soon as the priests lay hands on this hulking portrayal of sin, it will be slain in the presence of the Lord. It will be killed, not by the ones who brought it, but by the hand of another. Moses will kill the sacrifice, take its blood — the substance that gives the bull life and power — and paint it onto the horns of the altar with one little finger.

The bull's strength will be left dripping impotently from the symbol of the altar's power — its horns — as though the altar itself had just gored it. The bull's blood will also be poured around the base of the altar, as though causing it to "kneel" in defeat. Its oily fat — possibly symbolizing anointing and authority — burns on the altar. The rest of its carcass, meanwhile, will simply be incinerated outside the camp, like so much refuse.

The God of the tabernacle doesn't portray Himself as being willing to merely cope with or manage sin. Neither does He seem willing to ignore or minimize it. He puts a knife to sin's throat and kills it.

Does He forgive sin? Does He forget it? Yes, but only after it is brought kicking and screaming into the tabernacle to die.

Perhaps the sobering experience of taking these things to the tabernacle door and leaning into Christ's sacrifice will help us resist the next little calf of temptation that appears in our field. May we turn each one out before it grows horns.

*Be reconciled to God. For He made Him who
knew no sin to be sin for us, that we might
become the righteousness of God in Him
(2 Corinthians 5:20–21).*

Prayer: Lord Jesus, I tremble as I come to grips with sin. Let it move from me to You as it did with the sin offering. Let its power be broken as I lean heavily against You and name it for what it is.

Deeper Still

Read Galatians 5:16–26.
There is an ugly list of sins named in this passage. What happens in your heart when you call your own wrongdoing out by name? What happens when you picture Jesus taking it into the altar's fire to be consumed? Journal your thoughts.

Day 25

From Flesh to Fragrance

Before we begin, read Exodus 29:15–18

Having dealt with sin, God seems to need a demonstration of attitude from the priests next. Just how serious are they about living permanently with Him? To find out, He wants them to bring two rams to the altar next.

As with the bull, Aaron and his sons are to lay their hands on the ram's head, cut it in pieces, and burn it on the altar. The smoke rising from the fire creates "a sweet aroma, an offering made by fire to the Lord."

Male sheep (larger than ewes and with heads built for butting) are the leaders of the herd. When Aaron and his sons lay hands on it, the ram will become their surrogate or substitute (as the bull became in the sin offering). We might say an icon of leadership is being slain, cut into several pieces—head, legs, and innards—and tossed into the flames.

When Exodus 29:10–14 described the bull burning, it gave no reference to its smell, pleasant or otherwise. It's this first ram, its fat rendering with the roasting mutton, whose smoke gives off a fragrance the Lord enjoys.

Nothing will be left of the ram when they are done with it. The Hebrew word for "burnt offering" in these verses is *olah*—that which goes up. According to Henry

W. Soltau, it's "a sacrifice which entirely ascended in fragrance." (Soltau 1972, 367)

Everything that allowed the ram to lead itself or its flock will be consumed. What had once been most valuable about it—everything of substance, everything that had made the ram what it was—will be left in a tiny pile on the coals. Remarkably, God doesn't mention the ash in these verses. The residue grabbing His attention will be the lingering perfume of total devotion filling the rising smoke.

God wants us to be as all-in as the ram. If the priests' bath was like saying, "I do" in a wedding ceremony, then bringing the first ram is where we commit to "forsake all others and cleave only unto him." He wants all the different parts of us—our mind, our will, our emotions, our strength—completely and exclusively devoted to Him.

This total commitment may feel like giving up all that we are. God knows, though, that what remains will be transformed into an aroma that pleases not only Him, but all those in the courtyard.

Let us commit our whole mind and soul and strength to the Lord so He can convert us from flesh and blood into a sweet-smelling savor. May our fragrance fill the air and bless everyone in the tabernacle.

Hear, O Israel: The LORD our God, the LORD is one! You shall love the LORD your God with all your heart, with all your soul, and with all your strength (Deuteronomy 6:4–5).

Prayer: Lord God, help me commit myself wholly to You. Keep me steadfastly Yours so that my life is always rising like a pleasing incense before You.

Deeper Still

Read Mark 12:28–34.
What does it mean to you to love God with all your heart, soul, mind, and strength? Journal your thoughts.

Week Five

Discussion Questions

This week, we looked at the onyx stones and the gems on the breast piece. We washed at the laver, dealt with sin at the bronze altar, and began the process of consecration. Choose one or more of the following questions to consider on your own or discuss as a group.

1. Even if you don't see yourself as a "priest" in God's kingdom, what does it mean to you to know you always have access to His holy presence by means of the onyx stones on the shoulders of our Great High Priest Jesus?

2. Have you ever had that "I do" moment with God at the laver? If you have, share your story with the group. If you haven't, consider asking the others to help you symbolically step into those waters today.

3. Share your experience with coming to terms with sin in your life. Was it like hauling a wild bull to the altar for you? After all the trouble of bringing it to the Lord, how was your life different once that sin was "slain"?

4. The ram of consecration was completely consumed upon the altar. What does it mean to you to be "all in" with God?

5. Questions? Insights? Look for "A Place for Me in God's Tent" on Facebook and join the conversation.

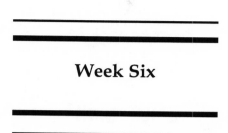

Week Six

Day 26

Can You Hear Me Now?

Before we begin, read Exodus 29:19–21

A second ram will approach the tabernacle door to play its part in hallowing, or setting apart, of the priests for service. Its blood, however, will be dealt with a little differently than the blood of the previous sacrifices.

Before sprinkling it around the altar, Moses is to paint some of the blood on the right ear, thumb, and big toe of Aaron and each of his sons. As each body part is marked, it will be dedicated to the Lord. Ears once open to anyone's conversation, hands once available for any activity, and feet once free to go anywhere will thus be reined in to serve God alone.

The blood touching the priest's ear will remind him to listen carefully to God. It won't be enough to simply hear what God says. He'll have to lean into God's wisdom with a determination to both understand and obey.

Before the blood on Aaron's ear has a chance to drip from his lobe, Moses will dab more on his right thumb. Aaron will have seen sacrificial blood touch the horns of the altar and pour at its base. He'll have painted it on doorjambs and lintels when the first Passover lamb was slain. This will likely be the first time he's seen it smeared on the flesh of a man.

As Aaron looks at his red and sticky digit, he may wonder what it all means. These hands are now destined for holy things — they'll hold the knife and slay the sacrifices, they'll change the showbread and trim the menorah's wicks, they'll be lifted in prayer and reach out to comfort. With this glaze of crimson, he'll know God has approved his hands for their appointed work. The same blood marking his ear to *hear* God's will, will counsel his hands to *do* God's will.

But Moses won't be done yet. He'll bend down and paint Aaron's toe — sending a message God wants him not just to hear and do what's right, but to go the right way as well.

Can you imagine Aaron's discomfort when he finds himself looking down on the top of Moses' head? There's a similar scene in the New Testament where Jesus, in John 13, bends over the feet of His disciples. Peter is uneasy with Jesus wiping his feet. I'm guessing both Aaron and Peter would rather have these two great men stand up again.

In the end, blood will only touch Aaron on his right side — the side associated with strength, honor, and blessing. It indicates everything he accomplishes ought to lean towards what is noble and praiseworthy and right.

Like Aaron and his brethren, we face choices at each fork along life's highway. Let's remember the splash of blood on our right ear and thumb and toe — the blood that set us apart as God's priests and disciples. It's a drop of blessing that keeps us pointing toward the Creator of the universe in all that we hear and do. It's the red badge of hope making it possible for us to live in His splendid tabernacle.

Your ears shall hear a word behind you, saying, "This is the way, walk in it," whenever you turn to the right hand or whenever you turn to the left
(Isaiah 30:21).

Prayer: Father, speak Your benediction over my ears and hands and feet. Cause them to ever lean Your direction.

Deeper Still

Read Proverbs 2.
This proverb implies laboring to find wisdom will not only give us greater understanding, it will bless both our work and our walk. How can you improve the intensity of your search for wisdom? Journal your thoughts.

Day 27

A Heavy Supply

Before we begin, read Exodus 29:22–28

The Master of the tent is almost finished describing the priests' hallowing process. It's time to fill their arms with good things.

God tells Moses to pile five basic elements in their arms—the ram's fat, kidneys, and right thigh, as well as bread and oil. Then they're to wave the whole stack before Him.

That may seem like a fairly simple directive, but consider how full their arms were going to be. The bread will be stacked in three forms—a loaf, a cake, and a wafer. On top of that, Moses will stack both of the ram's kidneys. It would be the final articles, however, that would make waving the whole mass quite a challenge.

Had God told Moses to toss a leg of lamb onto the pile, that would have been one thing, but He asks him to heave the leg of a full-grown ram into their arms. To this mass of mutton, he was to add all the lard he cut away from the carcass. (If you've ever tried losing weight, you'll know just how heavy fat can be).

This was the stack the priests were ordered to wave before the Lord. Can you picture it? I wonder if Moses would have to hide a snicker as they tried hoisting it without losing all semblance of dignity.

All in all, God presents a stunning picture of loading His ministers up. He gives them choice parts of the offering and supplies them with more than enough as they prepare to serve in His name.

Some people say that when God calls us, He also equips us. The tabernacle design certainly seems to bear this out. God's equipping, however, can often seem as unwieldy as the stack Aaron was supposed to carry. Whether we handle these great gifts with poise or ungainliness, to God we're heaving a wave offering before Him that He loves to see.

The gifts in the priests' arms aren't going to be for their own consumption. In verse 25, God tells them to toss the whole load into the fire except for the portion He designates for them to consume. Perhaps feeling the weight of it in their hands enables them to feel the full heaviness of their appointment.

As we take stock of what God's placed in our arms and draw its substance close, we too can gain an intimate realization of the responsibilities with which we're entrusted.

May the weightiness of these gifts neither frighten nor daunt us. Rather, may their bulk fill our hearts with confidence that what He calls us to do He will also enable us to accomplish.

Blessed be the Lord, Who daily loads us with benefits,
the God of our salvation! Selah
(Psalm 68:19).

Prayer: Oh Lord my God, how abundantly You enrich me for every good work. Help me handle Your gifts with generosity and grace.

Deeper Still

Read Jeremiah 31:10–14.
Notice how God promises to satisfy both the priests and His people. As you empty your hands of God's gifts in service to others, can you trust Him to fill your life with plenty as well? Journal your thoughts.

Day 28

Rest and Eat

Before we begin, read Exodus 29:31–37

So far, we've seen how God wants His ministers to be washed and clothed, dabbed and sprinkled and filled. As we approach the end of His description of the consecration process, God invites us to sit and share a meal with Him.

The portions that remained of the consecration ram are to be boiled for Aaron and his sons to eat. Bread would be included in the meal, as the priests stayed in the tabernacle for seven days to eat and to digest all that had happened to them.

Before the tabernacle, animal sacrifices went into the fire as an offering to the Lord. For the first time, the Host of the tent describes a part which would be reserved for human consumption. They would eat of the ram of consecration, from "those things with which the atonement was made, to consecrate and to sanctify them" (verse 33). In other words, the ram whose death provided them a place in the tent was going to become their food.

Eating of the sacrifice will not only qualify them for service, but for living in God's presence. Sharing in the meal would express their faith that guilt had been dealt with and they stood blameless and worthy to dwell with Him.

Consider the interplay between the one who would shed blood and the one for whom the blood would be shed. When the priests lay hands on the sacrifice, they'll identify themselves with the ram to be slain and become one with it.

When the ram enters the priests as food, it will touch them in return — this time on the inside — as it shares all its benefits with them. With each bite, eater and eaten become one.

What a perfect picture of Christ and His people. Hebrews 2:11 puts it this way, "For both He who sanctifies and those who are being sanctified are all of one, for which reason He is not ashamed to call them brethren."

If we choose to accept His invitation to dwell in His tent, a meal is prepared for us to share with Him. As we feed on Jesus as our sacrificial ram, we become one with all that He is.

He who eats My flesh and drinks My blood abides
in Me, and I in him. . . . he who feeds on Me will
live because of Me
(John 6:56-57).

Prayer: Lord, as I share in Your communion table, I confess that You are enough, that Your sacrifice was enough. You are my ram of consecration. Let me become one with You

Deeper Still

Read John 6:53-58.
The next time you receive communion, recognize your participation in the sacrifice Jesus made. As you and He touch in this meal, see yourself becoming one with Him. Journal your thoughts.

Day 29

Meet Him in the Incense Cloud

Before we begin, read Exodus 30:1-10

How appropriate that the Master of the tent would assign the altar of incense, framed in wood and covered with gold, to mark the spot where we would meet Him face-to-face.

Once their consecration is complete, the priests will be given a lofty new status to stand before the golden altar of incense. Nothing but the beautiful veil—its embroidered cherubim echoing the golden ones upon the mercy seat behind it—will separate them from the face of God.

A specially compounded mix of spices will burn day and night on top of the golden altar. A cloud of sweet fragrance will fill the holy place and seep gently through the tapestry into the Holy of Holies.

What is the incense supposed to represent? In Psalm 141:2 David sings, "Let my prayer be set before You as incense." In Revelation 8:3-4, an angel is given incense to "offer it with the prayers of all the saints upon the golden altar which was before the throne. And the smoke of the incense, with the prayers of the saints, ascended before God from the angel's hand." The smoke not only transports a sweet smell to the Lord, but carries the sound of His people's voices in prayer.

Notice something about the altar's measurements compared to the other furniture. While the top of the table of showbread is one and a half cubits tall (roughly twenty-seven inches), the altar of incense was a full two cubits (about thirty-six inches). While the priests, therefore, would have to stoop at the table to tend it, they'd be able to stand erect before the altar, positioned directly in front of the holiest part of the tabernacle.

What honor, what respect God allots to those who minister to Him. The ark of the covenant itself is a mere cubit-and-a-half tall, but when the cherubim are taken into account it likely rises to a height nearly level with man's face. Inhabiting the cloud of His people's prayers, enshrouded in incense, God demonstrates His desire to talk to man face-to-face.

God doesn't just *welcome* us at the altar of incense, He *longs* to meet us there. The incense of communication with Him isn't meant just for special occasions. Its smoke is to rise perpetually (Exodus 30:8). Day and night, morning and evening, God wants to inhale the pleasure of our company. Let us make His heart (and ours) glad by ministering at the altar of incense continually.

I love the LORD, because He has heard My voice and my supplications. Because He has inclined His ear to me (Psalm 116:1–2).

Prayer: Father, let me see Your face as You look on me, for it is beautiful. Let me hear Your sweet voice as well. I'm overwhelmed with gratitude for being invited to stand in Your presence and worship You face-to-face.

Deeper Still

Read Psalm 55:16–18.

"He shall hear my voice." Notice how determined the psalmist is. He attends to prayer often because he expects God to be paying attention each time. How confident are you that God will meet you in the incense cloud? Evening and morning and noon, He is always listening. Journal your thoughts.

Day 30

His Scepter Extended

Before we begin, read Exodus 30:1–10 again

There's an interesting difference between the altar of incense and the rest of the tabernacle furniture (aside from the obvious variation in dimensions and construction). The large brazen altar, the ark, and the table of showbread are each given four rings to accommodate their carrying poles. Though some diagrams illustrate the altar of incense with a similar set of four rings, here's what the blueprints say: "Two gold rings you shall make for it, under the molding on both its sides. You shall place them on its two sides, and they will be holders for the poles with which to bear it" (verse 4).

Some scholars have interpreted this to mean there were two rings *per side* of the altar, so that it hung square on the carrying poles. Henry W. Soltau, however, in *The Holy Vessels and Furniture of the Tabernacle* suggests there were only two rings, and these were attached to corners rather than flat sides. This would have allowed the altar to hang diagonally from the poles, its horns pointing to the four compass points as they carried it from place to place. (Soltau 1971, 96) When it rested inside the tabernacle, the altar would keep this orientation, directing one horn (a symbol of the altar's power) toward each of the four camps of the Israelites surrounding the tabernacle. (See Numbers 2 to read about the position of the camps.)

If this truly was the case, one of the first things someone serving at the altar of incense would confront on entering the holy place would be a horn from the golden altar.

Imagining this, my mind immediately goes to the scene of Esther approaching King Ahasuerus uninvited. Even though she was queen, her life would be forfeit unless the king responded by extending his royal scepter to her.

"Now it happened on the third day that Esther put on her royal robes and stood in the inner court of the king's palace. . . . So it was, when the king saw Queen Esther standing in the court, that she found favor in his sight, and the king held out to Esther the golden scepter that was in his hand. Then Esther went near and touched the top of the scepter" (Esther 5:1–2).

Tremendously relieved, Esther went on to make her request of the king who looked on her with mercy and granted her petition.

What a symbol of welcome the golden horn of the altar of incense makes, extending toward us like the scepter of Esther's king! We step into the holy place, and the air is sweet. Incense smoke softens every outline in the room. The only sound is the tinkling of bells hanging from the hem of the high priest's robe. Emerging from the fog, the golden horn of the altar of incense stretches toward us. Like the scepter of a king, it seems to announce, "Come forward, Child. You are already accepted, already welcome. Speak now. Father is listening."

Whatever we may think of ourselves, the altar of incense speaks its welcome to us. Before we even lifted the tent flap and peeked inside, He extended His scepter our way. Let us draw near with confidence.

> *Let us therefore come boldly to the throne of grace,*
> *that we may obtain mercy and find grace to help*
> *in time of need*
> *(Hebrew 4:16).*

Prayer: Lord God, You have shown me how ready You are to receive me. Let me worship You in joy as I bring my requests before You. Now, come on, my soul! Let this make you happy!

Deeper Still

Read Hebrews 10:19–23.
Combine the picture of God extending His scepter to you with the knowledge Jesus' blood "assures our entrance into the sanctuary." How does that increase your boldness before His throne? Journal your thoughts.

Week Six

Discussion Questions

This week, we finished with the process of consecration, sat down at table with the Lord, and stepped up to the altar of incense. Choose one or more of the following questions to consider on your own or discuss as a group.

1. While the first ram of consecration spoke of dedication in general terms (all or nothing), the second ram focused on a few particular areas of concern — the ears, thumbs and toes. Which has been of greatest concern to you personally — your listening, your works, or your ways?

2. When we lean on Jesus, we choose to identify with Him as our sacrifice. When we eat the bread of communion, it's as though He touches and identifies with us in return. Why do you think He chooses this type of relationship with us?

3. There are certainly times when our hearts make us bow or lie prostrate when appealing to God, but what does it mean to you that the height of the golden altar allowed His priests to stand upright when they faced Him in prayer?

4. Were you able to picture the horn of the incense altar stretched toward you as you entered the holy place? How did that increase your confidence you are welcome in His presence?

5. Questions? Insights? Look for "A Place for Me in God's Tent" on Facebook and join the conversation.

Part Two

The Place and We

In this set of devotions, we skip ahead a bit to find Moses explaining the tabernacle design to the people of Israel as they fashion the individual tent components. Just as each piece of the tabernacle—no matter its size, makeup, or function—has a particular place in the overall tent, we have a place in the larger family of God where we can feel at home.

Week One

Day 31

Out of Many, One

Before we begin, read Exodus 35:4–19

By the end of Exodus 31, God was finished talking about the blueprints for the tabernacle. Between that chapter and today's reading, there's been considerable drama. The Israelites played false with a golden calf, Moses threw a tantrum (well, he threw tablets anyway), God threatened to let them walk on alone, Moses talked God into giving them another shot, God had Moses carve out a new set of tablets, then finally sent him back down the mountain.

Today Moses stands before us to share God's instructions for the tabernacle. He begins with a list.

An exhaustive list.

Have you ever watched a speaker turn over page after page of a prepared address and wondered just how long this speech was going to be? I imagine the scene going something like that. Some people are forcing themselves to stay awake while others wonder what in the world this inventory has to do with them. *Come on, Mo. We don't all have gold or precious gems.*

During Exodus 12:35–36, the Egyptians forked over considerable plunder to the Israelites as they headed into the wilderness, but the loot came in a variety of forms —

not all of it precious. Wealthy Egyptians would have given more valuable goodies than the less prosperous.

Fortunately, Moses turns the page and reads off some less extravagant items. Yarn. Olive oil. Acacia wood. Can you hear the general sigh of relief rising from the crowd at this point?

I think it's interesting God hasn't required anything the people don't already possess. The New International Version translates verse five like this: "From what you *have*, take an offering for the LORD" (emphasis added).

Everyone may have something to contribute, but who could possibly take all these raw materials, all these bits and pieces of stuff, and fashion them into a proper dwelling place for God? In verses 10–19 Moses tells us, "All who are gifted artisans among you shall come . . . " and form and weave and nail everything together. It's not just the materials that are already in our grasp. The skills to transform them into the type of furniture and framework God wants for the tabernacle are likewise close at hand.

So, wood or gold, fabric or skin, yarn or goat's hair, contributions appear in every size and type. Spinners and weavers, artisans and craftsmen, everyone with a skill comes forward. Whether they bring materials or ability, none possesses all that's necessary to build the tent. It will take teamwork to accomplish God's purpose.

This principal hasn't changed. None of us can supply God with everything He needs to establish His kingdom on earth. Our contribution to the project may feel as glamor-free as a snippet of scarlet yarn. Yet if we make it available to skilled leadership, it can be woven into something as lovely as the tapestries and garments in the holy place. Our skill may feel as mundane as the ability to swing a hammer, but if we apply it to what others bring into the family, we can create an altar of holiness together.

This inability to satisfy God's purposes independently is deliberately conceived. I may be a "temple of the Holy Spirit" as an individual, but I'm also part of another, larger tent—a many-membered body created to be a dwelling place for God where all of us worship together. The apostle Paul hints at this in 1 Corinthians 12:11, where he says the Holy Spirit distributes His gifts to us individually.

This means our substance and abilities become increasingly valuable when we use them in community—when we join them with the gifts and skills of others. Together, and only together, we become what the apostle Paul calls "the measure of the stature of the fullness of Christ" (Ephesians 4:13).

> *But one and the same Spirit works all these things,*
> *distributing to each one individually as He will*
> *(1Corinthians 12:11).*

Prayer: Lord, I bring the gift of me to Your tabernacle. By myself, I don't have enough to build Your whole tent. Show me how to add my little bit to what Your other children are contributing and weave it in skillfully.

Deeper Still

Read 1 Corinthians 12:4–11.
Paul talks about different gifts and ministries and works as being appointed for the common good. How do you see your abilities being added to the talents of people around you? How does the impact of your contribution multiply when you use it in tandem with someone else's? Journal your thoughts.

Day 32

Willing Hearts

Before we begin, read Exodus 25:1–2
and Exodus 35:5, 20–29

When God first requested materials for the tabernacle in Exodus 25, He asked for offerings from willing hearts. Now that we've moved forward ten chapters, Moses is careful to pass His appeal for cheerful giving along to the people. "Whoever is of a willing heart, let him bring it."

I find it interesting these verses don't say *everyone* is bringing something, only those with willing spirits. To achieve this result, Moses doesn't give us a dissertation on why everyone ought to give. He doesn't twist arms or try to crank up an emotional response. He simply lists the necessary materials and gives everyone an opportunity to participate.

As we'll find out in Exodus 36:4–7, the response of the willing will be more than sufficient to get the job done. Apparently, the *bringing* isn't as important as the *willingness*.

Moses doesn't expect the people to try and stretch beyond their means. He tells them to give from what they have. In 2 Corinthians 8:12, the apostle Paul will echo the same idea. "If there is first a willing mind, it is accepted according to what one has, and not according to what he does not have." The important thing, he continues, is for each one to "give as he purposes in his heart, not grudgingly or of necessity; for God loves a cheerful giver" (2 Corinthians 9:7).

It's appropriate the word "offering" in both Exodus 25:2 and 35:5 is *terumah*—sometimes translated as a "heave offering." Giving is like lifting something up from our hearts to God. Have you ever had your heart so engaged in the giving of your substance or your skill that it felt easy to offer? Contributing out of duty or begrudging obedience makes offering more like pushing than lifting. It's hard to hoist what is heavy, but a willing spirit makes the lifting light.

Perhaps this is what Jesus talks about in Matthew 11:30, when He calls His yoke easy and His burden light. He found joy in pouring out His life for us, because He cheerfully chose to do so.

We needn't worry about the quality or quantity of our contribution compared to that of others. The list of materials God requires to build His dwelling place among us is broad and wide. It includes items anyone, male or female, rich or poor, might have in their possession. The question isn't whether our gift is precious or common, but whether our hearts are open and willing to using it as part of God's dwelling place.

Each of us has something God can use. If we lift it up from willing hearts it becomes part of a supply that will be more than enough.

So let each one give as he purposes in his heart, not grudgingly or of necessity; for God loves a cheerful giver
(2 Corinthians 9:7).

Prayer: Father, as I determine what I can contribute to Your tabernacle here on earth, help me zero in on what I can give cheerfully. Continue to expand the list of things I can offer with abandon.

Deeper Still

Read 2 Corinthians 9:6–15.

Paul names many rewards to joyful giving—sufficiency, abundance, more seed for our sowing. He also points out our giving doesn't just supply the needs of many, it increases the chorus of thanksgiving prayers rising to God. Can you think of times when your gift resulted in someone offering praise and thanksgiving to God? Does this multiply your own joy in having given? Journal your thoughts.

Day 33

Working in the Father's Tent

Before we begin, read Exodus 35:30–36:7

God had two particular men in mind to lead the tent construction. Today, Moses lifts up his voice and calls them out by name. Bezalel will be the primary artisan and Oholiab will be second in command.

These two are particularly qualified for the job. Moses lists their skills in engraving, designing, and weaving as well as their expertise in working with fine metals, woods, and gems. Within them rests all the know-how to construct the tent and all its furnishings. Given enough time, they could complete the work themselves. Except . . .

Moses reads one more qualification from their resumes — they are teachers (verse 34). They won't be carrying out God's plan alone. They'll be training up others to help build with them. Suddenly, the tent construction turns into a community barn raising of sorts. God wouldn't allow an elite few to supply all the materials for the tent when it was time to contribute, and He won't allow one or two people to receive all the praise for the beautiful construction now. "All Israel" was free to give of their means, so "all Israel" will have a role in building God's dream home.

Under the attentive training of Bezalel and Oholiab, those who begin the project as novices will grow in mastery. Those starting at a greater skill level will become virtuosos by the time it's finished.

Where do you rank yourself on the continuum of skill? Are you feeling hopelessly inadequate, atrociously inexperienced? Take heart. God doesn't just *accommodate* the less skilled, He *plans* for them. Remember how a willing heart was more important than the value of the actual gift in "Willing Hearts" on Day 32? It's the same for the skills we bring to God's work.

Exodus 36:2 says Moses called Bezalel and Oholiab "and *every* gifted artisan in whose heart the Lord had put wisdom, *everyone* whose heart was stirred, to come and do the work" (emphasis added). The word translated as "stirred" in this verse comes from the Hebrew *nasa*, meaning "lifted up." Serving, in other words, is one more opportunity to present a "heave offering" to the Lord.

How is your heart with the service you offer? Is the yoke easy and the burden light? Then you are welcome at the workbench with the most gifted of artisans. Look around for someone like Bezalel or Oholiab. Let them mentor you in the work and develop your skills.

Do your proficiencies and qualifications place you at the top of the skill ladder? Then examine your heart to see if God has placed an ability to teach within you as well. Who can you encourage to step up one more rung?

We don't just have a place at the *table* in God's tabernacle, we each have a place at His *workbench*.

Having then gifts differing according to the grace that
is given to us, let us use them
(Romans 12:6).

Prayer: Jesus, sometimes it feels my efforts don't go anywhere. Show me where I'm trying to go it alone and how I can better connect my gifts with what the rest of Your body is doing.

Deeper Still

Read Romans 12:3–8.

Paul gives a shortlist of gifts and ministries. Can you identify some of them as yours? Are there others you could name? Paul says if you've got a gift, just use it. Have you been holding any of them back? How could you get these gifts into gear? Journal your thoughts.

Day 34

Forming Attachments

Before we begin, read Exodus 36:8–18

The people are weaving the same linen and goat hair curtains we considered in "A Canopy of Protection" on Day 9 and "The Goat Hair Tent" on Day 11. When finished, all this fabric is destined to drape over the gold-covered walls of the tabernacle's inner rooms and cover it on three sides.

Neither set of curtains, however, is fashioned out of a single piece of cloth. Instead, the weavers are to create several separate panels and sew them together until they're left with a massive pair of each. Fifty clasps join the two linen halves together. Fifty more join the halves of goat hair curtains.

What's the purpose of all this sewing and clasping? According to verses thirteen and eighteen, it's so "it might be one tabernacle."

God has always wanted a unified people. In the Old Testament, He called twelve tribes to live as one nation. When they split in two, becoming Israel and Judah, He was heartbroken. Yet He would continually declare through His prophets they would reunite. In Ezekiel 37:22, for example, He says, "I will make them one nation in the land, on the mountains of Israel; and one king shall be king over them all; they shall no longer be two nations, nor shall they ever be divided into two kingdoms again."

The idea of two becoming one, in fact, began way back in Genesis 2:24, where God introduced Adam and Eve to each other the garden of Eden. After making them distinct, He told them to join as one flesh. This theme continues into the New Testament where, in Ephesians 2:14–18, the apostle Paul writes about Jew and Gentile becoming one.

Male and female, Jew and Gentile—great pairs of opposites, you might say. As different as they are from one another, they're to join together as one.

Just as the tabernacle won't work unless the great curtains act as one unit, God's kingdom doesn't function correctly unless we cling tightly together as a family, whatever our differences may be.

I'm reminded of this whenever I unroll the two outdoor roller blinds on my west-facing back porch. They are very much alike, yet complete on their own. If I want them to block the sun, I have to hook them together after I crank them down. Otherwise the wind rips them apart and carries them in separate directions. They've frustrated their purpose and I get no shade.

As members of the family of God, we can be carried off course like unfastened blinds if we fail to connect with those who feel "opposite" us. Troubles lift us by the corner and carry our hearts away from those who could otherwise stabilize us.

Building relationships isn't any easier than constructing those little fasteners for the two halves of the tabernacle. Curtains don't come with ready-made loops and clasps—they have to be sewn in and crafted intentionally.

God could have asked the people to weave each set of curtains out of a single piece of fabric. But He didn't. The tent is stronger because of the spaces formed between the loops and clasps — that little bit of difference between the two sides. Have you ever seen large banners with deliberately sliced holes in them? Wind is able to pass through without carrying the whole sign away.

Our attachments to one another are as important to us as a family as the loops and clasps are to the tabernacle. They strengthen us without binding so tightly that we lose our individuality. The collective tabernacle we become for God moves and breathes with the wind of His Spirit and our structure stays firm.

Now you are the body of Christ,
and members individually
(1 Corinthians 12:27).

Prayer: Father, You have placed me in a body. Give me the strength to stay connected to the other members even when it is hard — even when some of them feel like my opposite. Help me treat them like family, because they are.

Deeper Still

Read 1 Corinthians 12:12–20.

Are forming attachments difficult for you? What do you find most challenging in connecting with others? Is there a skill you could learn or develop that might make those attachments more secure? Has God appointed a Bezalel or Oholiab in your vicinity who could help you become more skilled in relationships? Journal your thoughts.

Day 35

Covering One Another

Before we begin, read Exodus 36:19

As we watch the craftsmen prepare the badger skins and red leather that will eventually be tossed over everything else, we have to wonder. With a layer of linen curtains *and* a layer of goat hair over the tent, why add more on top?

Let's step inside the tabernacle again and look up. Can you picture a seam of gold clasps and blue loops drawing a line in the ceiling? It's difficult to see, but above and running parallel is another seam, made of bronze clasps and plain linen loops. The two seams create a line of gaps in the tent. Openings that might expose its interior to the elements.

As the pieces of unstitched leather and unsewn skins drape over the clasps, they block the rain, insulate the tabernacle, and shield the precious furniture from encroaching wind and dust.

Bible versions differ on what type of animal skins constitute the uppermost layer. The New King James translates it as "badger" while other versions render the word differently—dolphin, hyrax, dugong, or porpoise. Though the ram skins are tanned and dyed, there's no indication the skins above them have been processed.

They're likely still furry — adding to the rain-deflecting/insulating properties of the covers.

What does this have to do with us?

When we gather together, we collectively form another type of dwelling place for the Holy Spirit — one the apostle Paul, in Romans 12:4-5, likens to a body with many members. A body which, like these great curtains, should be joined and knit together securely. Just as with the tabernacle, the places where we connect require some extra protection.

As part of God's dwelling place — as part of His family — we share a responsibility to cover each other, to protect the weak, to hover over the gaps of inevitable strain between us and help block the wind when storms come. Isaiah 32:2 says, "A man will be as a hiding place from the wind, and a cover from the tempest, as rivers of water in a dry place, as the shadow of a great rock in a weary land."

You and I may not feel tough as leather every day, but there's usually someone near us who is in a more fragile state than we. If I'm willing, I can be their covering of badger skin. As Romans 15:1-3 says, "We then who are strong ought to bear with the scruples of the weak, and not to please ourselves. Let each of us please his neighbor for his good, leading to edification. For even Christ did not please Himself; but as it is written, 'The reproaches of those who reproached You fell on Me.'"

A reproach is an expression of disapproval or disappointment. Imagine each of us as part of God's tent and His Messiah laying Himself over us like a giant badger skin. The shame and disapproval that should have fallen on us drops instead on His furry covering, where it slides off and trickles away.

This would be the role of His promised one, but we who dwell with Him are supposed to follow His example.

In imitation of Christ, we hover over each other to become as much of a shield for one another as we can.

He has given His life to cover us. Let us spend our lives covering each other.

A man will be as a hiding place from the wind, and a cover from the tempest, as rivers of water in a dry place, as the shadow of a great rock in a weary land
(Isaiah 32:2).

Prayer: Thank You for being my covering, Lord. Help me do the same for others. Even when I feel weak, let my eyes see opportunities to be a badger skin for someone else.

Deeper Still

Read Romans 15:1–6.

Paul reminds us doing something to build up our neighbor when we could have easily pleased ourselves is one way to follow Jesus' example. When was the last time you gave up your own pleasure in order to do good for someone else? What was the result for you and for that person? Journal your thoughts.

Week One

Discussion Questions

This week we saw the tabernacle could only be formed if many different people cheerfully shared their many different gifts with each other. We noticed our unity is secured by nothing less than the power of God combined with a spirit of mutual cooperation and concern. Choose one or more of the following questions to consider on your own or discuss as a group.

1. The tabernacle is made of separate parts working cooperatively as a single tent. What talents do you have that are particularly suited to be used for the common good? If you don't know what your contribution is, ask friends or members of your discussion group to help you identify it.
2. Have you ever brought an offering to the Lord out of a sense of duty or because you felt coerced to do so? What can you do to respond more appropriately to these pressures?
3. What methods have you found helpful for working cooperatively with people who are unlike you?
4. Questions? Insights? Look for "A Place for Me in God's Tent" on Facebook and join the conversation.

Week Two

Day 36

Less of Me

Before we begin, read Exodus 36:20–22.

The curtains and covers are finished. All we need now is a support system on which to hang them. Modern tents use ropes and poles for this purpose, but these won't do for the tabernacle. To carry this incredibly heavy load of fabric, Moses instructs the workers how to craft a gold-encrusted, wooden frame.

The frame is made of planks of acacia wood wrapped in gold—twenty for the north wall, another twenty for the south, and a few more for the west wall. (The eastern end will be the entrance so, for the time being, it remains open.)

These boards don't hold together just because they're standing side-by-side. They do so because the blueprints call for projections (translated as "tenons" or "pegs," depending on the Bible version) to extend from either side of each plank. This allows the boards to connect with one another. As they press together, a bit of each board hides inside its neighbor.

This locking mechanism transforms them from disparate slabs of lumber into walls solid and strong enough to support the massive canopy. To make the structure work, though, each board in the wall has to give something of itself to those alongside.

Developing relationships within this human tent family is like securing these boards together. It will cost each of us a little something. The apostle Paul echoes the same idea in the New Testament. "Therefore, as the elect of God, holy and beloved, put on tender mercies, kindness, humility, meekness, longsuffering; bearing with one another, and forgiving one another" (Colossians 3:12–13).

Putting on mercy, kindness, long-suffering, and forgiveness means extending the energy or substance I could have used for myself toward someone else. This kind of giving carves away at my edges, making more of the one standing next to me and less of myself. It's the love of God forming bonds of peace to makes us one people, one body.

Actually, the word translated as "tenon" or "projection" comes from the Hebrew word *yad*, meaning "hand." In a way, the self-giving qualities of the golden boards reflect our hands stretched out to each other — drawing one another close to become a wall capable of holding up God's beautiful tent for all to see.

Above all these things put on love,
which is the bond of perfection
(Colossians 3:14).

Prayer: Father God, when I give part of myself away out of obedience alone, it feels like subtraction. Plant the love You feel for my neighbor in my heart so my giving away becomes more like addition.

Deeper Still

Read Colossians 3:12–17.

Look at the list of things Paul tells us to put on. Which of these is the hardest for you? What does it require you to extend that you find so difficult? Ask the Lord to give you the key to stretching out your hands so you can be more like Him. Journal your thoughts.

Day 37

Silver Sockets, Silver Shekels

Before we begin, read Exodus 36:23–30

Though the boards will be secured into walls, the tabernacle is going to need a foundation to anchor the whole structure to the ground. Moses has the workers supply a pair of projections for the lower edge of each board, as well as for each pillar. These will snap into silver sockets on the ground. In order for every peg to have its own receptor, they'll have to create a total of one hundred of these sockets.

Silver is one of three metals mentioned in the tabernacle construction. It's the primary form of coinage in Old Testament times. When bartering isn't sufficient, coins are exchanged or redeemed for goods and services. This is probably why silver often carries an association with redemption.

Here in the tabernacle, the exchange rate for silver is high. It qualifies to redeem a human life from God's judgment. Coins, in and of themselves, aren't as valuable as human beings. They're only chunks of metal, after all. Their true worth is in what they represent.

Let's go back to Exodus 30:12–16 for a minute and remember how God told Moses to collect the silver.

"When you take the census of the children of Israel for their number, then every man shall give a ransom for himself to the LORD. . . . And you shall take the atonement money of the children of Israel, and shall appoint it for the service of the tabernacle of meeting, that it may be a memorial for the children of Israel before the LORD, to make atonement for yourselves."

When the census was taken, the people brought the price of their redemption to the tabernacle to have their names written in the Book of the Living. Each life was valued the same. The weak weren't worth less and the strong weren't worth more. Each one paid his "ransom" with one half shekel of silver and every ounce of that money has become part of the tabernacle.

The cost of redeeming the entire family of God rests in the silver-socket foundation of the tabernacle. Those little bits of coin will remain there as a memorial of every life belonging to God.

If you've never done so before, bring your life to the Lord and ask Him to receive it. The value of your life may feel as small as a silver coin, but God will plant it as a shining remembrance in His tabernacle.

He has sent redemption to His people; He has commanded His covenant forever: holy and awesome is His name (Psalm 111:9).

Prayer: Heavenly Father, here's my "half shekel" life. Redeem it so my name can be written in the Lamb's Book of Life.

Deeper Still

Read Psalm 130.
Have you felt the quality of your life wasn't worth much? Consider the "abundant redemption" mentioned in this psalm. Journal your thoughts.

Day 38

Melted and Molded

Before we begin, read Exodus 36:24–30 again.

The tabernacle designs don't tell us exactly what these sockets look like. Some experts suggest they're more likely flat on the bottom than spike-shaped, to accommodate setting the tent up in the inevitable rocky terrain of the desert. Whatever their shape, we do know one thing. They are heavy. According to Exodus 38:27, a full talent of silver makes up each one. Sources differ on the exact weight, but it's likely each socket weighs anywhere from seventy-five to one hundred and twenty-five pounds.

Remember how each person brought the same sized coin to the tabernacle to redeem for his life? Henry W. Soltau calculates it would take 6,000 coins to melt enough silver for a single talent. (Soltau 1972, 96) If true, that means each silver socket bears the weight of 6,000 lives.

We might say the sockets hint at a theme of many lives merging together. As it was with the curtains and boards, the idea of many becoming one will be repeated in the New Testament. In Romans 12:5, the apostle Paul likens God's family to a body with many members. In 1 Peter 2:5, the apostle Peter calls believers living stones in a single building.

A tent with many parts, a body with many members, a building with many bricks—all these analogies illustrate how we relate to one another in this family. They demonstrate a dwelling place for God made of individuals fitly joined together in peace.

It can be difficult, however, to believe our individual contribution counts for much when we consider the mass of silver around the tabernacle base. How big is a half shekel anyway? For that matter, how much does my gift matter in the mass of adoring worshippers who live in this tent with me? Where, in all this silver, is my little coin?

It's difficult to calculate our individual impact. If we contemplate the line of shining sockets, however, we can appreciate the cumulative effect of one hundred heavy talents functioning together.

What would the support be like if a few people decided their half shekel was too small to contribute? What would it matter, after all, if one socket consisted of 5,999 half shekels instead of 6,000?

Quite a lot, as it turns out, because God always insists on full and accurate weights (Deuteronomy 25:15). The idea that "almost" could be good enough wouldn't fly with Peter or Paul either. A body without a toe, after all, would be hobbled. A building missing a brick would lack soundness.

Consider how many times someone's apparently small contribution to your faith or well-being turned out to be life-changing. What if that person simply hadn't bothered to step up to the plate that day? Would you be where you are today?

Many times, all we need is a "half shekel" encounter with someone—a nudge, a hug, a kind word well placed—to go on with life. Many little touches melt together to big effect. We may not be able to tell exactly where one person's influence begins and another's ends in our life, but each person's participation is important in its time.

When each of us shows up to give what we have, the cumulative effect becomes the thorough undergirding represented in the tabernacle's silver sockets. So, let's be faithful to bring our full measure to the tabernacle. Who, after all, can tell where our half shekel might go?

If the foot should say, "Because I am not a hand, I am not of the body," is it therefore not of the body? (1 Corinthians 12:15).

Prayer: Lord Jesus, sometimes I feel I have so little to give. Help me remember my contribution is a vital part of a greater whole. May my small bit be part of Your full measure, pressed down, shaken together and running over in someone's life.

Deeper Still

Read 1 Corinthians 12:15–25.

This passage says the weaker, less presentable parts are given an honor the more presentable parts don't need. If God thinks this about members who otherwise seem less significant, what do you imagine He thinks of you? Journal your thoughts.

Day 39

Rings of Gold

Before we begin, read Exodus 36:31–34

You would think the tabernacle structure is sturdy enough by now, with boards linked together and walls secured to foundation sockets. Moses, however, is describing one more stabilizing feature God wants in His tent. Five poles — four short and one long — will run along each wall through golden rings attached to the boards' surfaces.

The side-by-side projections of the boards allow them to connect to one another in something of a "personal" relationship. The poles, on the other hand, create a more over-arching relationship between them by stretching across many boards at once. Made of the same gold-wrapped acacia wood as the boards, the poles give each wall additional strength.

Because there are five of them, my mind goes forward to the New Testament. In Ephesians 4:11–13, the apostle Paul says Christ appoints five leadership positions for His body on earth — apostles, prophets, teachers, evangelists, and pastors. These are given to us for our benefit, so we can grow into a firm structure he calls "the stature of the fullness of Christ." Like the poles in the tabernacle, leadership done well adds structural stability to the family of God.

When we resist or fail to honor our duly-appointed leaders, we become like tabernacle wallboards resisting their poles. Leaders are accountable to God for the way they carry the serious responsibilities He gives them. The author of Hebrews 13:17 takes the idea farther and encourages us to allow those in authority to accomplish their jobs "with joy and not with grief," because cooperation benefits us all.

It's easy to criticize and second-guess our leaders, or to think we could do their job better. We need to remember a couple of things, however. First, we aren't seeing the situation through the same cloud of stresses and responsibilities they are. Second, beneath it all, they're as human and fallible as any of us. Poles or boards, leaders or followers, we're all humble acacia wood at our core.

Humans have a tendency of failing to live up to expectations, but we can honor those in authority even when we don't think much of the job they're doing. How? By remembering what (or rather who) holds our leaders in place.

Look again at those rings holding the tabernacle bars in their positions. They're made of pure gold—a metal that speaks of God Himself. It's a detail that reminds us "there is no authority except from God, and the authorities that exist are appointed by God" (Romans 13:1).

Let our honor not be based on our opinion of leaders' personalities, qualifications or choices, but on who gave them the appointment. God promises to finish every good work He begins.

And whatever you do, do it heartily,
as to the Lord and not to men
(Colossians 3:23).

Prayer: Lord Jesus, I have leaders in my life who don't live up to my expectations. Help me honor them while still recognizing the human being they are inside. Grant me the ability to sense Your love for them, as You keep my trust firmly in You. Stir my heart to pray fervently for them.

Deeper Still

Read Colossians 3:23–24.

Do you have leaders with whom you find it difficult to cooperate? Can you serve more cheerfully if you focus on working "as unto the Lord" instead of unto the human? Journal your thoughts.

Day 40

The Team of Four

Before we begin, read Exodus 36:35–36

Bezalel and his crew are fashioning four wooden pillars and clothing them in gold. They'll be standing at attention between the Holy of Holies and the holy place to uphold the beautiful, cherubim-embroidered veil.

The number four usually hints at a worldwide theme. In Isaiah 11:12, for example, the prophet describes the earth as having four "corners." Revelation 7:1 speaks of it as having not only four corners, but four winds. Even today, we describe every earthly location in terms of its relationship to four cardinal directions (north, south, east, west). Why this worldly theme in the middle of the tabernacle?

The veil will hang from the upper parts of the pillars—what we might call their shoulders. As it happens, much of the tabernacle furniture is likewise appointed to be carried on shoulders—human ones. Poles will slide through golden rings to make sure people, not wagons, will support the holy things.

The author of Hebrews will describe the veil as somehow representative of the flesh of Jesus (Hebrews 10:20). As pillars in the house of God, we share a similar responsibility with our counterparts in the tabernacle. Instead of holding up a curtain, however, we put our shoulders under the story of Messiah and raise it high for people to see. Jesus encourages His disciples in John 12:32 with these words: "And I, if I am lifted up from the earth, will draw all peoples to Myself."

This gospel-lifting isn't a job we do alone. Just as each tabernacle pillar has the help of the others, we likewise carry the gospel together.

There are a lot of ways to communicate the Good News. In Luke 4:18–19, Jesus begins His ministry by claiming Isaiah 61:1–3 as His own. The passage lists many of the techniques He'll use to share His message. "The Spirit of the Lord GOD is upon Me, because the LORD has anointed Me to preach. . . . to heal. . . . to proclaim. . . . to comfort. . . . to console. . . . to give."

As I think about following His example, I see some things on this list I can accomplish. Other parts of it seem completely beyond me. For example, I am an introvert, so I find some social events more difficult than others. One year, for some strange reason, I agreed to sell cosmetics. Sweat poured by the bucket-load as I vainly made cold calls inviting people to my makeup parties. Potential clients stayed away in droves until I found someone else to do the gathering for me. Once I had folks in a classroom setting, my teaching gift cranked into gear, and my sales went through the roof.

We really are called to work together. Think about the way your body works when you want to comfort someone. It may be your arms actually touching their skin when you reach out to hug, but it takes the cooperation of your whole body to get them in position. Legs and feet bring you near. Muscles pull against bones to lift your arms. More muscles and tendons close those arms around the person and draw him or her in. One body part simply can't complete its mission alone.

Everything in God's tabernacle blueprints echoes the call for teamwork and interdependence. When we put our individually incomplete talents together, we can knock Isaiah 61 out of the park.

Together, nothing shall be impossible for us.

> *The Spirit of the Lord GOD is upon Me,*
> *because the LORD has anointed Me*
> *(Isaiah 61:1).*

Prayer: Lord, show me who I need to partner with to share Your gospel more effectively. Let my gifts bring the best out in that person as he or she brings out the best in me.

Deeper Still

Read Isaiah 61:1–3.

Which of these activities feel most like what you were "sent" to do in this world? Have you noticed someone in your circle whose gifts partner well with yours? Journal your thoughts.

Week Two

Discussion Questions

This week we noted the self-giving nature of the golden wallboards, the full measure of silver in the sockets supporting them, the divine placement of leadership demonstrated in the gold bars across the walls, and the joint responsibility of the four pillars upholding the veil. Choose one or more of the following questions to consider on your own or discuss as a group.

1. Can you think of a time when "putting on love" meant denying yourself some privilege, right or opportunity? What made it easy (or difficult) to let go of it for someone else's sake? Did the "subtraction" make you weaker or stronger in the end?
2. Only one half-shekel represented each life in the tabernacle's silver sockets. Can you think of a time you failed to give support because you felt your contribution was too small? What was the outcome?
3. What are some of the challenges you face in cooperating with those who are in authority over you? How can you improve?
4. Questions? Insights? Look for "A Place for Me in God's Tent" on Facebook and join the conversation.

Week Three

Day 41

Leading with Humility

Before we begin, read Exodus 36:37-38

As we turn from the veil and its four pillars at the entrance to the Holy of Holies, we find another drapery. Hanging from five pillars, this one marks the threshold between the duty and commotion of the courtyard and the place of fellowship with God at His table. It's less elaborately decorated than the veil and is called the "door" of the tabernacle.

Let your gaze travel up fifteen feet to the tops of the pillars. Notice those gold caps they're wearing? Some Bible versions call these "chapiters" or "capitals," but the Hebrew word for them is *rosh* or "head." You might say the pillars' heads are crowned with gold.

Pillars. Strong, supportive and prominently placed. As with "The Rings of Gold" on Day 39, they make me think of leadership. Even without their crowns, the columns must be ponderous. That extra gold on top must threaten to make them top-heavy. Maintaining their stability will require secure bases at their feet. If they lean the slightest bit, if they acquire the tiniest tilt, they'll block or further narrow the way into the holy place. Fortunately, there's a fitting counterweight for the added glory on their heads — the bronze sockets at their feet.

Because of its association with the altar and its sacrifices, bronze is often seen as symbolic of judgment. The color alone is reminiscent of the altar's fire.

The pillars' crowns are like the extra honor and authority leaders carry. These special benefits, however, can threaten their upright stance if they aren't firmly grounded. Those who rule must continually remember who fixed them as pillars in the first place. Whatever it may look like, they don't hold their place because of personal virtue, power, or fame. As we noted before, "there is no authority except from God, and the authorities that exist are appointed by God" (Romans 13:1).

Leaders can ground themselves by remembering God will be the ultimate judge of their performance. Humility is a force as strong as a bronze socket and a fitting foundation for keeping ourselves plumb with what's right.

Does this mean those of us without a formal title are off the hook? Afraid not. If we look around, we're likely to discover someone is following each one of us. Do we have children or grandchildren? Do we have friends looking to us for guidance? Are we sharing our expertise with someone? In these or any number of cases, we are leaders, shepherds, guides for someone else. The message for the pillars, therefore, is for us all.

Whoever we rule, and however we do it, let's follow Jesus' advice in Luke 10:20 not to rejoice in our great authority and honor, "but rather rejoice because your names are written in heaven." Whether we lead with a title or without, let's balance the gift of esteem with humility until the day when we're free to toss those heavy crowns at His feet (Revelation 4:10).

He had equal status with God but didn't think so
much of himself that he had to cling to the
advantages of that status no matter what
(Philippians 2:6 MSG).

Prayer: Father God, You have put people in my life who look to me for leadership and guidance. Keep my feet steady in humility as I strive to point the way to You. Keep me upright so pride doesn't tip me sideways and block someone else's way to closer fellowship with You.

Deeper Still

Read: Philippians 2:3-11.

When God gives us influence over others, it's easy to see where they're going wrong. Sometimes that knowledge makes us want to force them to do the right thing. In this passage, Paul notes even though Jesus was in the form of God and had all power and authority, He took on the form of a servant. How might you be more of a servant to those under your care? Journal your thoughts.

Day 42

A Box of Memories

Before we begin, read Exodus 37:1-9

When God first gave Moses the blueprints for the tent in Exodus 25, He described the ark of the covenant before He described anything else. For some reason, Moses discusses the curtains, walls, pillars, and door hangings before he introduces the ark. But here we are at last.

Elaborate curtains, woven and sewn into enormous swaths, will soon hide the innermost room under their wings. Timber planks plated with gold will stand around the Holy of Holies like sentinels locked arm-in-arm. It's as if each piece is destined to turn its most glorious parts inward to focus its attention on the modestly-sized, gold-plated box in the tabernacle's core.

In Moses' day, the heart of most religions centers on an image created in a deity's likeness. Worship in the tabernacle, however, revolves around a glamorized wooden box. What is it about the ark that makes it the rightful core of our attention?

Perhaps it isn't so much the ark as what's hiding inside. Today's reading doesn't specify the contents, but other passages do. In Exodus 16:33, Moses reserved some of the miraculous manna in a jar while they were still in the wilderness. Deuteronomy 10:2-5 repeats the story of Moses climbing Mount Sinai. It says he built a wooden box there to hold the tablets God etched with the Ten Commandments.

Now that the more formal ark has been constructed, these items can be transferred into it. Another item will join them in Numbers 17:10. Aaron's rod—so often used to demonstrate the miraculous—is brought back to life, sprouting leaves and buds and flowers. Hebrews 9:4 tells us it, too, will rest inside the ark.

The addition of these items transforms the ark into a time capsule of sorts—a treasure box of souvenirs commemorating the family's history and identity. Why these particular memories, though?

The Ten Commandments are like a set of "house rules" any well-functioning family might have. Families are bound together by shared stories as well. The rod, once placed in the ark, will memorialize a close call over family division. The manna testifies of God's faithfulness to show up right on time with the miraculous.

Past family victories are worth remembering and celebrating. They revive hope that today's troubles will be overcome as well, and the family will yet survive every challenge.

In part, I think, remembering is much of what the golden treasure box is about. We strain to stay united as individual pieces of God's tabernacle, but our curtain panels pull against their stitches, snapping like thunder in the gale of life lived together. We try to hold tight, but our gilded boards rub and squeak against each other in stormy winds that rattle our connections.

In times like these, let's zero our attention in on the golden box. The collection of proofs hiding within it will help us remember—remember when God's provision showed up though there was no opportunity to plant or harvest; remember when He spoke from the cloud of chaos in the midst of our terror; remember when resurrection came to a long-dead stick.

"Forget what pulls and pushes," the box seems to sing. "Forget what annoys and threatens. Look to Me and remember. What I've done for you and with you before, I will do again."

But these things I have told you, that when the time comes you may remember that I told you of them (John 16:4).

Prayer: Father, revive in me the memories of troubles successfully conquered in the past. Remind me of times You brought unity out of what looked like permanent division. If I can't find stories of victory in my own experience, then let the history of Your family Israel strengthen me.

Deeper Still

Read Philippians 4:6–9.
Paul recommends we keep thoughts that are true, noble, just, pure, lovely and of good report at the forefront of our minds. How does this kind of remembering help you through stressful situations? Journal your thoughts.

Day 43

Fellowship at the Table

Before we begin, read Exodus 37:10–16

Bezalel and his assistants are back at the workbench. This time, they're building a piece of furniture commonly known as the table of showbread. As with many of the other items, its framework is wood and the laminate gold.

At only one-and-a-half cubits in height (about twenty-four inches), it seems more like a coffee table than a dining table to the modern eye. What is short by today's standards, however, is just right for biblical times where people don't sit in chairs while eating, they recline on cushions. The table is low, but its top is broad— approximately eighteen by thirty-six inches. Plenty of surface area for twelve heavy loaves of bread.

Mealtime culture during Moses' day was a bit different from what some of us experience today. David H. Stern, in his *Jewish New Testament Commentary*, says gathering around the table was meant to be more than a social event. For religious Jews of the day, it's an opportunity to discuss the *Torah* (God's Word). Why? Because religious studies without social interaction does society little good. On the other hand, if the main socializing event of the day—mealtime—doesn't include a discussion of the things of God, "it is a sign that religious truth has not penetrated deeply into the life of the individual." (Stern 1995, 227-228)

When a family gathers for a meal, they're expected to do more than interact with each other socially. They're to use the time to discuss God's words of wisdom. This way the family can "chew" on its meaning together.

The table of showbread is a piece of furniture promoting a combination of physical, social, and spiritual food. What better place for it than one of the tabernacle's most intimate rooms?

Doesn't this put a whole new spin on the New Testament adage not to forsake gathering together? Assembling as a family isn't just about hearing God's message. Nor is it simply for catching up with each other's news. It's even about more than communion wafers or bits of bread. It's an opportunity to interact with one another, to share our perspectives on the Scriptures and to grow together in understanding.

My favorite worship meetings have been those where people lingered after the "business" of church was done and shared with each other what they gleaned from the service. We are like fellow loaves on God's table, sharing nourishment with one another through our insights.

Hebrews 10:24-25 says, "And let us consider one another in order to stir up love and good works, not forsaking the assembling of ourselves together, as is the manner of some, but exhorting one another, and so much the more as you see the Day approaching."

Stirring one another up. Exhorting one another. Letting the life in our loaf give energy to someone else at the table.

Do you feel you're not enough of a Bible scholar to participate in this table talk? No worries. Our contribution doesn't have to be profound. A good meal, after all, isn't all steak and potatoes. Bring your little salad or big desert and let each of us contribute to the conversation. Perhaps we can stir one another to greater love and more good works.

And they continued steadfastly in the apostles' doctrine and fellowship, in the breaking of bread, and in prayers (Acts 2:42).

Prayer: Lord, help me take a bit more time when I come to Your gatherings. Embolden me to enter into conversation with someone else and share what I discovered that day.

Deeper Still

Read Acts 2:42–47.
The disciples seemed to have spent considerable time eating together. What do you think happened around the table? What was the result of all this fellowship? Journal your thoughts.

Day 44

The Wonder of Almond Wood

Before we begin, read Exodus 37:17–24

Do you hear the sound of a hammer? Not the heavy clang of an iron monger, but the gentle tap of a gold smith transforming the soft metal into a work of art. It's Bezalel and his associates crafting a lampstand in the shape of a tree. It looks nothing like the acacia with which we've become so familiar. Every detail of the lampstand says it's an almond tree.

What skill, what artistry to urge the shape of ornamental knobs, flowers, and "bowls made like almond blossoms" from its branches. If *Holman's Illustrated Bible Dictionary* is correct, the "knobs" we're looking at are very likely almond nuts. (Brand, et al. 2003, 999) It means this glowing bush is flush with buds, blossoms and fruit all at once. What kind of tree can do that?

The Hebrew word for almond wood is *shaqad*, which means to watch, keep awake, or hasten. According to *The Bible Knowledge Commentary*, the almond was known as the "awake tree" because it bloomed in late January. (Dyer, Walvoord and Zuck 1985, 1131) That made it among the first of the trees in Israel to bud and bear fruit each year. Heralding spring before it arrived, it became a symbol for the watchfulness of God (see Jeremiah 1:11–12).

I wonder if Moses felt a bit of *déjà vu* when he saw this glowing almond tree, alight with its seven flames, finally take its place in the tabernacle. The last time he had seen a burning tree was in Exodus 3:7–8, when the Lord spoke with him in the desert. "I have surely seen the oppression of My people who are in Egypt, and have heard their cry because of their taskmasters, for I know their sorrows. So I have come down to deliver them."

With the lampstand, God establishes a glowing reminder in the tabernacle that He is finely tuned to His people, ever awake and aware—more awake than an ordinary almond tree could be.

As we stand in the glowing light of the lampstand, how fabulous to realize that this is the God we serve. Perpetually aflame and awake, continually lighting our darkness, superior to both time and nature, He is alert to doing exceedingly, abundantly more than we can ask or imagine.

As we noticed in "Let There Be Light" on Day 8, we are represented in those six side lamps. Their orientation is an important detail to remember when life seems to get dark around us. Each one points toward the central lamp. Set apart from its brethren, this light is sometimes called the western lamp because it always faces the ark of the covenant. (Edersheim 1994, 125)

If we see our neighbor's gaze shifting away from the light of God, let's be vigilant to help them to turn back to the light of His Messiah. With our eyes enlightened by His Holy Spirit, we won't be afraid of the dark.

He who keeps you will not slumber. Behold, He
who keeps Israel shall neither slumber nor sleep
(Psalm 121:3–4).

Prayer: Lord, sometimes it feels like You don't see me, but the burning almond tree in the tabernacle, the golden lampstand, reminds me You are awake and watching over me all the time. Light up the dark places in my heart and let me see You.

Deeper Still

Read Psalm 121.
What does it mean to you to know God "shall never slumber nor sleep" as He watches over you? Journal your thoughts.

Day 45

The Light of the World

Before we begin, read Exodus 37:17–24 again

Let's hang around the light a bit longer, shall we? Some Bible versions call this bit of tabernacle furniture a candlestick. It's fueled by oil not wax, however, so "lampstand" is a more appropriate title.

Because creation was finished in seven days, the number of limbs on this tree hints at something perfect and complete. Each of its seven branches bear a small, almond-shaped lamp filled with olive oil, but the central light is distinct from the others. As we noted last time, all other lights train their attention on it, while the middle flame points toward the Holy of Holies. From the shaft of this inner branch, each of the others arise. Additionally, when the priests begin tending the lampstand, they'll use a coal from the brazen altar to light the central lamp before lighting the other six from its flame.

The distinctiveness of the middle stem of the tree-like lampstand strongly hints at the coming Messiah. Prophets would speak of one who would be called the "Branch." Coming from the root of Jesse, He would rise up to be King (see Isaiah 11:1, Jeremiah 23:5 and Zechariah 3:8).

In John 8:12, Jesus would identify with this Messianic branch by calling Himself the "Light of the world." As though pointing to the menorah's side branches in Matthew 5:14, He'd also call *us* the light of the world.

In *The Holy Vessels and Furniture of the Tabernacle*, Henry W. Soltau makes an interesting comment. "The light sent forth by this beautiful vessel, though proceeding from seven lamps, yet was but one light; the lamps are never said to send forth *their lights*, but *light*; the oil ministered to each was the same, and is always specified as oil for *the light*, not for the lamps." (Soltau 1971, 79) In other words, there are many lamps, but only one light.

It reminds me a bit of how lighthouses work. When they first appeared on our coastlines, only a single light burned in each one. The distance they could shine toward ships at sea was limited. A single flame has only so many lumens. All that changed when Augustin-Jean Fresnel developed his special lens in 1822. He ground one thousand pieces of glass into precisely shaped prisms and set them in order around a central flame. He called these prisms "lights" even though they only magnified the actual source of illumination. With this new arrangement, lighthouses could stretch their beams all the way to the horizon, twenty miles out to sea.

Doesn't that sound similar to our relationship with Jesus? He operates as our High Priest, tending our lamps as we cling to His branch. He fills us with the oil of His Holy Spirit, setting us aflame with His light. Set in order around Him, we magnify His goodness to those struggling around us.

Our individual lamps aren't very bright, but because we gather together, we never shine alone. Like separate prisms in a Fresnel lens, each of us takes the light of the Christ and shares it from a different angle. Together we magnify His glory, scattering His light as far as the horizon.

Sometimes we sing about letting our little light shine, but that's an inadequate picture for what's really going on. We glow next to other flames on His lampstand, not so much as plural *lights* of the world, but as magnifiers of His central *Light*.

> *I will also give You as a light to the Gentiles, that You should be My salvation to the ends of the earth (Isaiah 49:6).*

Prayer: Lord, let me draw my fire from Your flame and shine with the lamps You have placed near me. Together, help us magnify You.

Deeper Still

Read Ephesians 5:8–14.

Paul warns the Ephesians to avoid participating with darkness. Cooperating with the gloom means keeping our light hidden. What are some situations where you are *in* the darkness and struggle not to be a *part* of it? How do you keep your lamp lit? Journal your thoughts.

Week Three

Discussion Questions

This week we considered the importance of staying grounded in humility as leaders of others. We looked at the ark as a box of memories and examined how we could make for a more complete communion by discussing the Scriptures with each other. Then we marveled at the way many lamps shine with one light from the lampstand. Choose one or more of the following questions to consider on your own or discuss as a group.

1. Even if we don't have an official title, someone is usually following us. List a few people who are counting on you for guidance, encouragement, care or support. How can you keep yourself grounded in humility as you serve them as a leader?
2. The ark, in part, was a time capsule of the people's faith-history with God. Can you identify a time when remembering God's past faithfulness was key to overcoming discouragement?
3. Do you have a group of friends with whom you can discuss the Scriptures? How has considering the Word from someone else's perspective helped you better understand it?
4. Can you think of a time you worked as a team with other believers to shine the light of Christ to

someone? How was it different from presenting that light by yourself?

5. Questions? Insights? Look for "A Place for Me in God's Tent" on Facebook and join the conversation.

Week Four

Day 46

Heavy Lifting

Before we begin, read Exodus 37:25–28

Bezalel and the other artisans are occupied with one final bit of goldsmithing—wrapping the plain wooden frame of the altar of incense in glory.

From a satellite view, the altar of incense is four-square—about eighteen inches wide and deep. From a street view, however, it rises higher than almost any other object in the holy place (aside from, perhaps, the lampstand, because we don't actually know its size). At about thirty-six inches, its surface is above even the flat part of the mercy seat inside the Holy of Holies.

Let's think of this a minute. If we position ourselves at the altar and pull the veil aside, the ark of the covenant stands before us. Though the flat surface of the mercy seat is a few inches lower than the altar, its two grand cherubim rise from it. If they don't surpass the height of the altar, I think they surely match it. Here we stand, before the very place God said He would meet with man in Exodus 25:22—between the cherubim.

Face to face with God. What an honor. I think the extra height of the golden altar reflects not only how high a calling it is to worship God, but how great our responsibility is to maintain communication with Him.

As honorable a place as it is, prayer can be a solitary ministry. The golden rings attached to corners of the altar are a reminder, however, that God might ask us to pick up the responsibility at any time. One person would never be able to move the altar alone. The same soft and pliable gold laminate that made the altar so beautiful also makes it heavy. God knows this so He provides carrying poles so we can lift it together.

Have you been there? Serving at the altar of incense and realizing you couldn't lift the burden of prayer alone? Life can challenge us with troubles that bring us to our knees. Those are the times we need help getting our shoulders under prayer.

There are few better examples of this type of intercessory teamwork than in Exodus 17:8-16, when Israel was fighting against Amalek. As long as Moses held his staff aloft (as though calling on God in prayer), Israel prevailed. If he allowed the staff to drop, they began to fail. It wasn't a job Moses could handle on his own. A nation was at stake, but Moses could only hold his arms up for so long. That's when Aaron and Hur stepped up and supported his arms.

Think of Moses as representative of the altar of incense — his prayers rising like smoke before the Lord. Then picture Aaron and Hur standing at His side, putting their arms under his — as though slipping poles through the rings of the altar — to support him during the battle.

There's no indication Moses asked for help. Aaron and Hur apparently just saw the need and stepped in. Moses, for his part, expressed no shame in accepting their aid.

When our work at the altar requires some heavy lifting, let's neither be embarrassed to ask for nor ashamed to receive help. God gave the tabernacle furniture a built-in way to be carried. He's blessed each of us with a similar design.

We are confident that as you share in our sufferings, you will also share in the comfort God gives us (2 Corinthians 1:7 NLT).

Prayer: Open my eyes to those who need help around me, Father, and show me the way to get my shoulders under them for support. When others offer to help me, grant me the humility to let them hold me up.

Deeper Still

Read 2 Corinthians 1:3–7.

This passage talks about allowing the comfort we received in hard times to translate into comfort for others. How can your own experience with trouble guide you in finding ways to support others in similar difficulties? Journal your thoughts.

Day 47

Everything Stops When the Smoke Rises

Before we begin, read Exodus 30:34–36 and 37:29

Now that the golden altar is being prepared, let's go back a bit and consider the compounds making up the incense that will fill the holy place with fragrance.

Four spices are being pounded and blended together for this purpose. Stacte, onchya, galbanum, and frankincense. Some of these are unfamiliar and there's some debate on what fragrance each one offers. Whatever the specifics, every spice contributes something different to the final aroma in the tabernacle.

As we noticed in "Meet Him in the Incense Cloud" on Day 29, the golden altar is a place of prayer. When we gather to worship the Lord together, we are like incense spices coming together. Each brings his or her own fragrance into the room.

One brings a sweet atmosphere of joy to the gathering. Another carries in the sharp scent of mourning. Some approach with a heart filled with bitterness, while others draw a soft quietness into the room. Blended together, our separate aromas become a full-bodied fragrance—an incense so precious to God, He reserves it for Himself alone.

Psalm 100:4 invites us to come into His gates with thanksgiving and enter His courts with praise.

Sometimes, however we simply can't do that by ourselves. We need to let ourselves steep in the smoke of others as we minister at the altar of incense.

If I stand at the altar alone on a given day, my prayer might be all bitterness and sorrow. Exposed to the aroma of others, the smoke of my intercession takes on new dimension. I hear how you pray, note what you ask for, and see how you approach God. My perspective gradually changes. Someone else's joy drifts my way. The sharp pain in the voice of others joins mine, and I take comfort my sad incense isn't rising alone. The consolation I couldn't find alone floats toward me from those praying nearby.

Alfred Edersheim describes what used to happen in the temple (the permanent structure which eventually takes the tabernacle's place) at "the time of incense." When everything was ready, someone would strike a large instrument called the "Magrephah," sending an alert throughout the temple grounds. Cleric and layperson alike hurried from every part of the compound to stand in their places of service or worship. Once everyone's attention was focused on the holy place, the priest poured incense into the golden altar's fire. Smoke filled the holy place as everyone in the compound simultaneously stopped what they were doing and prostrated themselves in silent prayer. (Edersheim 1994, 127–128)

Imagine it. Silence. Stillness. It was as though the entire temple held its breath as God inhaled the fragrance of His people's prayers.

The book of Revelation describes a similar moment in heaven. In Revelation 8:1–5, silence reigns "for about half an hour," as an angel fills a golden censer with incense and offers it with the prayers of the saints upon heaven's golden altar.

Are you worried God isn't listening to your prayers? Let yourself be infused in the smoke of others praying at the altar. Let God inhale your fragrance as part of that full-bodied bouquet He loves, and remember what's going in the throne room. Hear the silence. Watch all heaven come to a stop as God focuses His attention on the smoke of your intercession.

And the smoke of the incense, with the prayers of the saints, ascended before God from the angel's hand (Revelation 8:4).

Prayer: Lord, give me an opportunity to pray with other believers. Let me be part of the smoke going up at Your golden altar. Help me hear the silence as You listen to my prayers.

Deeper Still

Read John 11:1–44.
In this story of Lazarus, Jesus purposely prays out loud so the crowds can hear Him. Though He could have accomplished His purpose without doing so, He chose to pray in the presence of others, allowing His faith to infuse theirs. Has your faith been strengthened during group prayer? Could your faith strengthen others in similar situations? Journal your thoughts.

Day 48

The Bronze Centerpiece

Before we begin, read Exodus 38:1–7

The banging of hammers shifts our attention again. We turn away from the altar of incense, leave the muffled quiet of the tent, and cross the courtyard to a spot barely inside the tabernacle gate. Here the artisans are plating another wooden altar with metal. This time, the armor they're giving it is bronze.

Planted like a monolith, taking up more acreage in the tabernacle complex than any other piece of furniture, the brazen altar is so large, thirty-five of the incense altars could be stuffed inside it with room to spare. Once finished and in service, no one will be able to enter or leave the grounds without confronting it, without hearing the crackle of its fire, without smelling the charred flesh of the sacrifice burning, always burning, upon it.

The death of a sacrifice will be the centerpiece of the courtyard—its rising smoke the visible proof an acceptable substitute is burning in the altar's fire. Testifying to the power of its role, Bezalel directs the bronze-workers to hammer four horns—generally symbolic of strength and authority in biblical times—onto the corners of the altar. (DeHaan 1955, 72)

No ministry in either the holy place or the Holy of Holies can take place unless a sacrifice is burning there.

The ignition source for the lampstand and the fire for the incense come directly from the burning coals consuming the bloody sacrifice in the courtyard.

Later, God will augment the message of the tabernacle with promises from His prophets. They'll announce the coming of a Messiah who will be a more fitting sacrifice for the altar. Isaiah 53 in particular paints a picture of Him as someone afflicted, bruised, led as a lamb to the slaughter, on whom God would lay "the iniquity of us all."

Like the bronze altar in the tabernacle, Jesus' death on a cross has become the centerpiece for our faith. His life of perfect faith, obedience, and love prove He is the only acceptable offering to take our place on God's heavenly altar. He is the Lamb of God who takes away the list of charges written against us.

If we are His dwelling place, His tabernacles on earth, we can't pussy-foot around the centerpiece of His death. It must be part of the message we share, because it holds the key to understanding why any of us has access to His presence. The altar's horns reflect the strength of this message. While the apostle Paul calls the cross foolishness to those who are perishing, in 1 Corinthians 1:18 he says it is likewise the power of God to us who are being saved.

Jesus didn't die to impress us with His bravery or to inspire us with His ability to endure abuse and pain. He died because sin needed to be punished and He didn't want us punished with it. Let's make sure we aren't afraid to make that known.

For I determined not to know anything among you
except Jesus Christ and Him crucified
(1 Corinthians 2:2).

Prayer: Heavenly Father, show me where I am being too timid about sharing the message of the bronze altar.

Deeper Still

Read 1 Corinthians 15:12–19.

Paul points out the necessity of Christ's death. Jesus didn't *send* sin to the grave, He *took* it there with Him. Imagine the scene as Christ hand-delivered sin to its final resting place. Journal your thanksgiving to Him for this incomparable gift.

Day 49

Mirror, Mirror

Before we begin, read Exodus 38:8

Today, we find workers preparing a bronze bowl and basin that will be positioned between the altar and the door of the tabernacle. Bezalel and his assistants are creating it from the mirrors of "the serving women."

Some authors suggest these mirrors symbolize something about vanity, but I think it's something else.

We find these women "at the door" (the entrance to the holy place), hovering near the site of deepest worship. I see them lingering just as close to the presence of God as they are allowed to come. To me, this doesn't suggest they are struggling with vanity. The door of the tabernacle is a smoky, bloody, busy place. It doesn't seem like a great spot to show off your glam. I think these women use mirrors for the most basic of purposes — identifying blemishes they need to remove.

No other item in their possession likely contains as much bronze as their mirrors. Contributing them to Moses is giving large. We don't know how many women are at the door the day Moses asks for more bronze, but their contribution is sufficient to complete both the laver and its basin.

Many mirrors merge together into the shape of a bowl and basin. As individuals, they only had the power to *reveal* blemishes. Once they're combined, they can hold the substance capable of *removing* blemishes. If we think of the bronze altar as symbolizing *God's* judgment of mankind, mightn't the bronze laver illustrate mankind's responsibility to judge *himself*? (Epp 1976, 79–80)

The New Testament will liken God's Word not just to mirrors, but to water. Ephesians 5:26 describes how Christ cleanses His church "with the washing of water by the word." James 1:23 speaks of the Word as a mirror into which we look to examine ourselves.

In a way, the artisans fuse many personal reflections into a larger cooperative one in the bronze laver and basin. We create a similar benefit when we gaze into the mirror of God's Word and examine it from our different perspectives.

Looking into it alone can be a scary thing. Some of the imperfections we discover when we gaze at ourselves may be easy to cleanse on our own. Confronting larger issues can be daunting without allies. We need trustworthy friends alongside when there are difficult judgments to make about ourselves. A loving community can help us be more successful with our struggles.

If you've had success with the behavior change I need to make, I want you as my cheerleader. If you're facing the same strong temptations I've already managed to defeat, you could sure use my support.

Looking into the laver with all the angles its many mirrors provide, helps us see our own reflection more clearly. Here, our diverse life-experiences and insights draw the cleansing waters of Scripture into a pool. They rise into a healing power as we encourage one another around His fountain.

Confess your trespasses to one another, and pray for one another, that you may be healed (James 5:16).

Prayer: Father, it's so embarrassing to confess my faults to someone else. My heart would rather hold its own counsel, hide its own shame, and deal with its own issues. Show me someone safe to practice this kind of self-exposure. Make me a safe partner, as well, for someone else struggling with the view from Your laver.

Deeper Still

Read James 5:13–20.

Confession isn't the only thing we do with partners. James lists other activities as well. Any of them could be done individually, but power increases with combined forces. Have you tried opening your heart to anyone else in this way? If it didn't go well, would you be willing to try again? Journal your thoughts.

Day 50

Bridal Skirts

Before we begin, read Exodus 38:9–16

The tabernacle complex won't be surrounded by pointy posts of timber and rigid wooden rails the way a military stockade might have been in the old west. It's to be wrapped with soft curtains made of finely twined linen.

Linen is the fabric of clothing. When it's wound around the tabernacle, it will seem to dress the entire community in a giant robe—or perhaps a white festal garment more like a wedding gown.

The people of the Old Testament tabernacle wouldn't have thought of themselves nationally as a bride at this point. The apostle John's vision on the island of Patmos hundreds of years later would establish the idea forever. He says the promised Messiah, the Christ, will have a bride who is not one person, but many. In Revelation 19:7–8, a voice from heaven declares, "For the marriage of the Lamb has come, and His wife has made herself ready. And to her it was granted to be arrayed in fine linen, clean and bright." Then the voice defines just what the white fabric refers to. "The righteous acts of the saints."

How does Christ's bride wrap herself in good works? Second Corinthians 5:21 says we were *made* righteous when Jesus took our sin to the cross. We *dress* righteously when good works flow freely from our grateful hearts.

These good works are, in part, a sign of our heart condition, an indicator of whose bride we are, an identifier of our personhood. Jesus explains in Matthew 7:15–20 that a tree is known by the fruit that comes from it. John the Baptist takes the Pharisees to task in Matthew 3:8 when he warns them to "bear fruits worthy of repentance."

Righteous acts of love, joy, peace, longsuffering, kindness, and goodness are the fruits of the Spirit of God within us (Galatians 5:22–23). They drape us with qualities befitting our status as His tabernacles. These loving actions are alluring as a bridal gown. They draw the attention of the needy, create trust in the wary, and promise relief to the lost. They urge the wanderer to come into God's refuge, find welcome, and sit at His banqueting table. We're supposed to be known as a family for such acts.

It's going to take more than a smattering of good works to do the job. Just look how much time the weavers spend at the loom to make enough fabric to surround the tabernacle. They're creating two, fifteen-cubit lengths of fabric (about seven and a half yards each) for the eastern end of the courtyard and a fifty-cubit swath (about twenty-five yards) for the western end. That's nothing, however, compared to the north and south sides of the courtyard. They're each going to need a whopping one hundred cubit stretch of linen (roughly half a football field long).

It would be one thing if the plans allow them to be stitched together from smaller pieces as the curtains were, but they don't. Each of these grand spans must be woven individually.

Can you imagine such a project? Can you feel the aching backs of the weavers as their shuttles race back and forth across the loom day after day? Can you see the steadily rising pile as they fold and refold the linen until it's long enough to disconnect it from the loom? How much do you suppose each mound of fabric weighs?

This is the sort of weaving and weaving of righteous works that makes me think of Marley's ghost in *A Christmas Carol*. In describing to Scrooge what the heavy chains he wore were, Marley said they were the product of evil deeds. "I made it link by link, and yard by yard; I girded it on of my own free will, and of my own free will I wore it."(Dickens 1911, 28)

Piece by piece, Scrooge and Marley forged their "courtyard fences" with unrighteousness. We, on the other hand, are to weave goodness, kindness, and benevolence by the bolt, until its shining splendor stretches round our courtyard. Let's make garments attractive enough to beckon the wanderers to come in from the wilderness.

And to her it was granted to be arrayed in fine linen, clean and bright, for the fine linen is the righteous acts of the saints (Revelation 19:8).

Prayer: Father, show me how to increase the works of goodness and kindness I'm currently engaged in. Then fill my mind with an abundance of inspiration for even more good works I could do.

Deeper Still

Read 1 Peter 2:9–12.

Peter reminds us of our role as a royal priesthood includes thinking and acting in love. It's not enough to abstain from evil, we're to actively brighten our robes with a diligence to do works of kindness and mercy and benevolence. What are some ways you can activate good works in your life—the kind that bring glory to God if they're noticed? Journal your thoughts.

Week Four

Discussion Questions

This week we stepped up to the golden altar as a team and appreciated the many spices making up its incense. We considered the importance of communicating the message of the bronze altar, the need to help one another deal with the blemishes in our reflections, and the challenge of being a community known for good works. Choose one or more of the following questions to consider on your own or discuss as a group.

1. Describe a time you benefitted from a team effort at the altar of incense. Did you play a supportive role, like Aaron or Hur, or were you more like Moses in that incident? What difference did teamwork make in the outcome?

2. The incense on the altar contained a mixture of spices. Have you noticed a benefit from having the "aroma" of other people's prayers around you? How does it affect your own ability to pray?

3. Though most of us know the importance of confessing our trespasses to God, we're also instructed to confess to one another. Have you found that easy or difficult to do? What might improve your ability to do so?

4. Did the good works of others play a role in attracting you to the Lord? How big a factor was it in drawing you to Him?

5. Questions? Insights? Look for "A Place for Me in God's Tent" on Facebook and join the conversation.

Week Five

Day 51

Crown of Glory

Read Exodus 38:17

It's time to get up from the loom and give our backs a stretch. As you massage that crick in your neck, allow your gaze to travel upward fifteen feet to the tops of the fence posts being set up.

Bezalel and his silversmiths are busy accessorizing the posts with three silver components—hooks, bands, and capitals. The capitals are the metal caps covering their tops. Just below them, silver hooks protrude from each post, ready to accept the silver bands or rods that will run horizontally between them. Once all this bling is connected, it will add stability and support for the great weight of linen. (Strong 1987, 20–21)

Take a moment to spin slowly in place and appreciate the final effect. As you track the entire circumference of the fence's toppers, it looks like a spiked halo of silver encircling the courtyard. It reminds me of Isaiah 62:3. "You shall also be a crown of glory in the hand of the LORD, and a royal diadem in the hand of your God."

We already associated silver with redemption in "Silver Sockets, Silver Shekels" on Day 37. While the shekels represented a fairly low cost for the worshipper who brought it, other elements in the tabernacle show the true price of writing a person's name in the Book of Life.

A spotless life substitutes for a blemished one. As long as the tabernacle survives, animals go into the flames on the brazen altar, sacrificing their lives for human ones. None of them goes willingly.

One day, however, the promised Messiah will come and *choose* to give what the animals could only be forced to offer. In the New Testament, Jesus reveals Himself as the Lamb of God. It will not only be His *will* to go to the cross, but His *joy*, because His motivation for dying will be love (Hebrews 12:2).

In John 15:13, Jesus says, "greater love has no one than this, than to lay down one's life for his friends." So, while we think of silver as representing redemption, let's also consider its relationship to love.

Take another look at the shining crown encircling the courtyard. The gleaming white metal runs in two directions — upwards (in the crown-like capitals) and sideways (in the horizontal hooks and bars). Jesus referenced two great commandments in Matthew 22:37–40. "You shall love the LORD your God with all your heart" and "love your neighbor as yourself." The love of God carries a vertical aspect similar to the fence's capitals, while loving our neighbor resembles the bars running between them.

If the linen curtains are a reminder to be busy performing righteous good works, the silver jewelry holding them up should remind us to be motivated by love.

The strength of the rods demonstrates the type of resilient love the Master of the tent wants between His family members. In John 13:35, Jesus would make it clear this was to be a defining feature of our lives together. "By this all will know that you are My disciples, if you have love for one another."

The world may seek us out for miraculous works. They may find our eloquent words or prophetic nature impressive. They may appreciate our good works. But they will only truly believe we belong to God by the strength of our ties to one another.

These kinds of relationships are costly. They reflect a Christ-like affection—one that loves the Judas who betrays, the Peter who disappoints, the Nicodemus who can't understand, the Martha who isn't listening, and the *me* who keeps failing and falling. It suffers long and seeks ways to be kind. It resists provocation, refuses jealousy, and trumpets the accomplishments of others. As 1 Corinthians 13:7 says, it "bears all things, believes all things, hopes all things, endures all things."

As precious as the fire-tried silver stabilizing the courtyard is, this priceless love can be inconvenient and uncomfortable. But if we can learn it with our tabernacle family, we'll be better qualified to love those outside our tent.

By this all will know that you are My disciples
if you have love for one another
(John 13:35).

Prayer: Lord Jesus, help me with this kind of strong, resilient love. You have such experience with loving those who disappoint or fail You. Put that love in me and teach me how to keep hold of it through every storm that tries to yank it from my hands.

Deeper Still

Read 1 Corinthians 13:1–8.
You've likely heard or read this passage many times. Take a moment now to read it slowly as you ask the Lord

whether one of these verses is key to loving someone in your circle. Journal your thoughts.

Day 52

Courtyard Gate

Before we begin, read Exodus 38:18–20

Let's step outside the courtyard for a moment, as though we're approaching for the first time.

At first, all we see is a strip of white fencing surrounding the tabernacle complex. Above it, we can just glimpse the top of the dark tent in its interior. To discover anything more about what's behind the fence, we have to locate the way in. We walk along the northern, western and southern walls, but one patch of linen looks very much like any other. We pick a spot and try to crawl underneath, but can't. There will be no burgling our way in. The fabric is stretched too tight. Rounding the final corner, we come to the eastern wall. And there, everything changes.

A stunning tapestry meets our eyes. It's about twenty-two feet long and woven through with scarlet, purple and blue threads. Hanging from four pillars and centered on this portion of the fence, there's no mistaking that this is "the gate"—the appointed way into the tabernacle.

Three colors herald the nature and purpose for the Messiah to come. Red hints at His humanity. Purple heralds His royalty. Blue reveals His heavenly origins. In John 10:7–9, Jesus identifies Himself with this doorway.

Remarkably, the tabernacle's Designer places the job of weaving this prophetic piece of cloth into human hands.

God is still building a tabernacle today. This one isn't made of cloth and wood, it's made of living stones. The job of showing the way into God's house is still in our hands today. We tell the story of the gate by weaving our several gifts together.

Each of us sits at a slightly different position at the spiritual loom, working with hands particularly skilled for our portion of the tapestry. All our colors must mingle in correct proportions to illustrate the fullness of Christ to the world.

Some people seem especially talented at testifying to Christ's righteousness, good works and perfect nature — as though spinning vast quantities of the white linen threads. Others seem intent on making sure there's enough red thread for the job — constantly focusing on making His sacrificial death clear. Other weavers love to work the purple threads. They tell stories of His kingly authority and encourage their listeners to trust and obey. Finally, there are those who love nothing more than threading their needles with blue yarn. They can't help embroidering mysteries of His heavenly origins into their conversations.

Do you feel like you sew better with some colors than others? No worries. We weave the grand story of the gate together. Then, like pillars in the tabernacle, together we hold it high.

I tell you the truth, I am the gate for the sheep
(John 10:7 NIV).

Prayer: Lord, I thank You that I don't have to use the same story threads as anyone else. Thank You for the special skill You have given me to tell my part of the gate's story.

Deeper Still

Read Isaiah 40.

Notice how many different aspects of God this voice in the wilderness describes. Rough places are leveled and the crooked is made straight. He's revealed as ruler, creator, judge, healer, comforter, and encourager. Which of these threads do you normally find in your hands when you tell others about Christ? What fascinates you about the color you tend to use when weaving your story? Journal your thoughts.

Day 53

Our Vested Interest

Before we begin, read Exodus 39:1–7

As we look over the shoulders of the artisans fashioning the priest's ephod, we can't help but notice its similarity to the fabric of the courtyard gate and the door to the holy place. Threads of blue and purple and scarlet weave beautifully through fine-twined linen in them all. An extra bit of bling, however, shines from the ephod—narrow strips of gold woven in like threads.

Heavenly gold weaving through earthly linen. What does that make you think of? To me, it's another beautiful illustration of God entwining His life into ours. Another picture of Emmanuel—God with us.

Let's look more closely at how Bezalel and his helpers are assembling the ephod to see what its construction might mean for us.

Because verse four speaks about coupling it together at the shoulders, the vest is likely made of two pieces of fabric. When finished, one piece will drape over Aaron's breast while the other covers his back. The gold threads add just a bit of weight to the vest, making it almost hug him both fore and aft. What a reminder of Isaiah 52:12. "For the LORD will go before you, and the God of Israel will be your rear guard."

Gold isn't the only element giving heft to the ephod. Two onyx stones, etched with the names of the twelve tribes, are "enclosed in settings of gold" and attached to its shoulder seams.

I'd always pictured these settings as flat platforms of gold with little prongs holding the gems in place — something like the diamond in an engagement ring. The word translated as "settings," however, comes from a Hebrew word meaning "plaited work." Tiny braids of gold, elaborate filigree, perhaps even delicate, golden netting are holding the stones in place. Imagine the shimmer it adds to the inscribed names.

The resting place for this glorious vesture is astonishing. Moses will drop the vest over the head of Israel's high priest. When that happens, Aaron will become, in a sense, a human body clothed with Emmanuel. It's as though the designs of the priests' clothes point forward to New Testament times when followers of the promised Messiah would become known as His "body" and would be clothed with God's character, power, and authority.

Jesus would show by many signs and wonders that He was Messiah come in the flesh — the Great High Priest who would hold that office forever. As members of His body, we go wherever our High Priest goes and His clothing drapes over us. The family names carved into the onyx stones, therefore, rest on our shoulders too — a sign we share a responsibility to pray for our brethren.

I don't know about you, but those stones can weigh heavy sometimes. We don't always get to pick and choose who we ought to pray for. The onyx stone lists include the entire family and it seems God finds all of them precious enough to set in gold.

To be honest, I carry some names into God's throne room way more easily than I carry others. There are people I bring gladly to the Lord. Others I sometimes wish I could ignore.

As a result, I often neglect to pray for some of the people God places in my sphere. I may throw encouraging words and friendly platitudes their way. I may even toss money into their ministries. But pray for them with any fervency? Not so much.

The ephod reminds me it shouldn't be so. We can't keep some of the names on the onyx stones and shake off others. God frames each one's importance to Him in precious, gold filigree. We *are*, after all, our brother's keeper.

> *The voice of your brother's blood cries*
> *out to Me from the ground*
> *(Genesis 4:10).*

Prayer: Lord, help me to care more for the people You've put in my life. Let me experience Your love for them so I may be more diligent to pray.

Deeper Still

Read Philippians 1:1–18.

The word "you" in this beautiful opening prayer in Paul's letter to the Philippians is plural. He was praying for the whole community even though, in verses 15–18, he mentions some had been acting like enemies. Who have you been avoiding praying for lately? Journal your thoughts.

Day 54

Designer Pocket

Before we begin, read Exodus 39:8–21

It's time to accessorize the ephod.

The garment-makers weave another length of gold-laced linen, fold it in half, and stitch up its two sides. The end result is a pocket about eight inches square. When attached to the ephod, it will rest squarely over the priest's heart. Depending on which Bible version you read, this part of priestly vestment is called a "breast piece," "breastplate," or "pectoral."

According to James Strong, however, the translation from Hebrew is "spangle" or "glistening." (Strong 1987, 107) It's not just the gold threads running through the fabric that make the pocket shine. Twelve different gems, each set in its own golden filigree, decorate the front of the pocket in a rainbow of colors.

When we think of a breastplate, we often picture stiff Roman protective gear. The one God styles for His priest, however, is more flexible and certainly much smaller than the military variety. (Strong 1987, 106–107) Its modest dimensions cover little more than his heart.

This spangly addition to the ephod makes me think of the fancy pockets sewn onto name-brand clothing. Decorated with the maker's logo, these pockets function as fabric billboards, advertising the brand wherever the bearer goes.

The best logo designs convey something about the maker—a mood, an atmosphere, a feel for what the company represents. The Nike swish, for example, conveys motion, signifying a company that's all about athletics. The final two letters in the official FedEx logo form a right-pointing arrow, creating a subtle message they'll get your package "there." A logo's color, design, shape, and even the order of its components, help tell the consumer (at a conscious or unconscious level) what to expect from the business they represent.

The "logo" on the ephod's pocket consists of twelve distinct stones, each representing one of the tribes. The breadth of variety demonstrated in the lives of His children advertises the many facets of God's nature. God designs this "company logo" with a collection of living stones to tell the story of what He's like.

Experts disagree on the modern equivalents for some of these gems, but each possesses its own color, clarity, and properties. Someone standing in front of the high priest can easily appreciate how well, yet how distinctly, each stone handles the light passing through it.

The stones themselves, I imagine, find it more difficult to fully comprehend their own effect. I might look at you from the outside and think, "How beautifully Christ's light shines through that one." When I look at myself, on the other hand, my position in the breastplate limits my ability to clearly assess my impact on the world. My stone seems duller than yours from my perspective. Less colorful. Less amazing.

Scripture warns us not to envy one another. It inevitably leads to dissatisfaction. Better to trust the one who assigned our stone its place and knows how to make us shine. He composed His breast piece with a full complement of living stones. Each of us has our own characteristics and is placed just so over His heart. Together, we advertise a full and accurate picture of Christ on the earth.

Let your conduct be without covetousness; be
content with such things as you have
(Hebrews 13:5).

Prayer: Lord Jesus, help me believe You have made me as lovely as the other gems on Your breastplate. Let me trust You to shine through me in the way You intended.

Deeper Still

Read 1 Thessalonians 5:12–22.
This passage is all about esteeming one another and actively pursuing what is good for all. How does having this mindset help keep you from fixating on comparisons? How can you "pursue what is good" for someone who's been a source of jealousy for you? Journal your thoughts.

Day 55

Robe of Blue

Before we begin, read Exodus 39:22–26

Remember how we first discovered the tabernacle from the inside out? As the high priest's garments are developing, Moses takes us from the outside in. He described the glorious outer layers first and now he moves one layer inward to show us the blue robe.

He doesn't tell us what type of fabric to use (though we can probably assume it's linen). Neither did God name it in Exodus 28:31–35, where He first introduced the robe. We know the robe only by color . . . and by sound.

Pomegranates made of blue, purple, and scarlet thread bounce against alternating gold bells on its hem. Because the fruit is fashioned from yarn, the bells will ring with soft tones rather than harsh clangs whenever the priest takes a step.

As the priest enters the otherwise quiet holy place, the understated music of the robe will enter with him. While he ministers out of eyesight, the gentle carol of bells will be reassuring the people someone is busy serving on their behalf before the Lord. When he leaves the holy place, the song of the jingling vestment will counteract the chaotic noise of the courtyard with soothing notes of heaven.

The peacefulness of the robe makes me think of Isaiah 42:2 where the prophet describes the Messiah. "He will not cry out, nor raise His voice, nor cause His voice to be heard in the street."

When Jesus appears in the New Testament, He doesn't often raise His voice, yet He makes Himself not only heard but understood. The gentle music of His ministry tenderly woos us to "taste and see that the LORD is good" (Psalm 34:8).

We take a cue from the blue robe when, in our urgency to see a person safely home in God's tent, we are careful not to raise the pitch of the gospel by resorting to finger-pointing. Isaiah 30:15 reminds us it's "in returning and rest" people are saved.

Jesus shares His good news this way in Matthew 11:28–30. "Come to Me, all you who labor and are heavy laden, and I will give you rest. Take My yoke upon you and learn from Me, for I am gentle and lowly in heart, and you will find rest for your souls. For My yoke is easy and My burden is light."

Let's go and do likewise—allowing our gentle conversation to soften the noise of everyday life for others.

The work of righteousness will be peace, and the effect of righteousness, quietness and assurance forever (Isaiah 32:17).

Prayer: Lord Jesus, may people sense the peace of Your blue robe when they meet me. Fill my words with gentleness and flavor them with reassurance and hope, so others may be drawn to You.

Deeper Still

Read James 3:17–18.

James mentions several aspects of Godly wisdom in his letter. Which ones are your strong suits and in what areas are you weaker? How might you soften the sound of some of the bells on your robe? Journal your thoughts.

Week Five

Discussion Questions

This week we studied the need to stay firmly bound together in love. We reflected on which "colors" we most often weave into the way we share the gospel, noted the importance of praying for one another, and considered how uniquely our stone shines on our Great High Priest's breast piece. Finally, the blue robe reminded us to keep our conversation as appealing as the gentle sound of the golden bells at its hem. Choose one or more of the following questions to consider on your own or discuss as a group.

1. Have you experienced groups of believers who seemed to be active with good works, shared plenty of accurate, inspiring teaching, but clearly held little concern for one another? How did that affect you? How can you help strengthen the bonds between your own circle of friends?
2. The courtyard gate was filled with color. Which threads do you tend to focus on when weaving the story of the gospel? Blue, red, purple or white?
3. How do you deal with the tendency to compare yourself with others? Take some time to point out to each other the beauty you see in their particular "stone" on Christ's ephod.

4. When does your conversation tend to get harsh when discussion the gospel with others? How might you soften your tone?

5. Questions? Insights? Look for "A Place for Me in God's Tent" on Facebook and join the conversation.

Week Six

Day 56

Real Love Costs

Before we begin, read Exodus 39:27–29

Touring the tabernacle from the inside out, took us from its most glamorous elements to its least. The breathtaking ark of the covenant gave way to the common dust and simpler beauty of the courtyard. Our examination of the priestly garments has taken us from the outside in, yet it's still moved us from most elaborate to least. We peeled back the glittering ephod and breast piece to see the more common blue robe. Now that Moses is drawing our attention to the innermost layer, things have gotten — dare I say it — downright bland.

Plain, unadorned linen makes up the tunic, turban, and trousers. Only the sash is given any color at all. These clothes rest closer to the priests' skin than any other article of clothing. Nothing will lie beneath them but the priests' utter nakedness.

Covering a person's birthday suit brings my thoughts to Genesis 3:7, when the world's first man and woman realized they were exposed and naked before God. They tried covering their shame with leafy attire, but God wasn't satisfied with the result. He slew an animal to cover them with its hide, in what some consider the very first sacrifice.

Leaves simply weren't costly enough to settle accounts for their guilt. Plants, after all, don't lose much by having their leaves stripped off. They'll just grow new ones. An animal must spill its blood and die to give up its hide.

As early as Genesis 9:4, God was explaining the importance of blood. It contained the life of an animal and only something *with* life can be a substitute *for* life. When a human life is in the balance, only something with blood can pay a sufficient price to stand in for him at the altar.

Why, then, is bloodless plant material satisfactory as a covering for the priests' nakedness?

While a variety of plants can provide usable material for clothing, none of them gives up as much as the flax plant when producing linen. Harvesters don't simply cut it off at the base as they might with wheat or hay. They pull it up by the roots, then further traumatize it by submitting the stalks to processes called scutching, retting, and heckling (more about this in Part 3, but yes, these are just as delightful as they sound). All in all, you might say flax is a plant which is familiar with suffering. It gives up its life to become linen.

For the lesser priests, tunics, trousers, turbans, and sashes make up their entire wardrobe. For the high priest, they are undergarments. For particular sacrificial duties — on the Day of Atonement, for example — he'll have to strip down to this humble layer before performing them. He'll lay aside everything that shows his great status and glory.

As with the high priest of the Old Testament, there are times we must lay aside the benefits of office or status to serve God's people properly. The fate of the flax reminds us that underneath it all, love is going to cost us.

Jesus knows the price for such humility. He knows what it means to lay personal glory aside in order to do the Father's bidding. He'll be a fitting comforter and confidante as we follow His example, so let's fearlessly go and do likewise.

By this we know love, because He laid down His life for us. And we also ought to lay down our lives for the brethren
(1 John 3:16).

Prayer: Lord Jesus, the idea of suffering doesn't appeal to me much, but I want to be like You. Let Your love grow in me until the desire to serve overwhelms my distaste for hardship.

Deeper Still

Read 1 John 3:16–20.
What can you lay aside to bring benefit to another person in a way that would please God? Journal your thoughts.

TERRY MURPHY

Day 57

Dressed to Serve

Before we begin, read Exodus 39:27–29 again

Last time, we noticed only one splash of color in the priests' linen outfits. The sash has the same blue and scarlet and purple threads we saw running through the gate, door, veil, and ephod. This relatively tiny addition to their clothing, gives priests from the highest to the lowest status a connection to the tabernacle in which they serve.

Lower priests will get used to wearing only this modest nod to the holier parts of the tent. I wonder how humbling it will feel to Aaron, though, when he has to strip down to his "skivvies" for certain duties. How will the congregation react when they see their holy man remove his vestments one by one and lay them aside to scoop ashes?

Have you ever felt humiliated for someone else when you watched them do something that seemed beneath their dignity? The apostle Peter would in John 13. The one he knows as the Messiah, the Christ, the Son of the living God, lays aside His outer garments and girds Himself with a towel. As He humbly washes the disciples' feet, Peter is apparently not only uncomfortable with the situation, he is horrified.

I think I can relate. I'm okay when someone else washes my hair. And I think I could deal with someone washing my arms or legs. (Well, as long as I was in the hospital, maybe.) But my feet? I don't even get a pedicure very often because I don't want anyone looking at my crooked toes and down-to-the-nubbins toenails, much less touching them. I mean, really. Salon workers wear rubber gloves for a reason.

Yet in the New Testament we see Jesus touching His disciples' feet with loving and totally bare hands. He wants a crack at the everyday dust they'd accumulated — the unavoidable soil picked up by sandaled feet doing what they were created to do. Once done, He tells His followers in John 13:14 to care for each other in the same way.

Washing hints at forgiveness. As we go about our daily lives in this world, its dirt *will* rub off on us. We'll step on its splinters and stub our toes on obstacles. The dirt and the sores constantly remind us how imperfectly we walk.

Sometimes we have trouble forgiving ourselves for our stumbles and uncleanness. That's when we need friends who will humble themselves, touch our less-appealing places, and pour the loving waters of mercy and forgiveness over them.

Whatever robes of office God has appointed us in this tent family, may we always be ready to lay them aside for the linen garments of servanthood on His command. Our duty is not only to God but to His children, our brothers and sisters of the tabernacle.

Let this mind be in you which was also in Christ Jesus
(Philippians 2:5).

Prayer: Lord Jesus, keep me mindful of the linen undergarments You've appointed for me. Make me quick to take up the towel and stoop to serve Your family.

Deeper Still

Read Philippians 2:1–8.
Paul mentions holding others in higher esteem than ourselves. Who would benefit from a sign of your esteem right now? What are some ways can you "gird yourself with a towel" and serve them? Journal your thoughts.

Day 58

Holy to the Lord

Before we begin, read Exodus 39:30–31

The artisans are completing their final bit of work. The turbans for the priests will all be linen, but the high priest's cap will need an additional ornament—a gold identifier engraved with "Holy to the LORD." Aaron and those who follow him will be completely dedicated to and set apart for God's purposes.

The gold tiara attaches to Aaron's turban just above his forehead, the symbolic center of a person's purpose, will, and mind. It's the place we decide who will or will not rule over us—the seat of either stubbornness or resolution.

I find great hope in having the words etched into gold and tied on with a blue cord. To me, this indicates Aaron will have supernatural help to live up to the words on his crown—a supernatural help I expect the Lord to share with me.

After all, God would promise to help the prophet in Ezekiel 3:8–9, when he'd have to deliver some particularly difficult words to some particularly stubborn people. "Behold, I have made your face strong against their faces, and your forehead strong against their foreheads. Like adamant stone, harder than flint, I have made your forehead; do not be afraid of them, nor be dismayed at their looks, though they are a rebellious house." It was as though God tied a golden tiara to Ezekiel's forehead to strengthen his resolve.

Aaron will eventually transfer this crown to his son Eleazer. In Numbers 20:25–28, it begins its journey passing from high priest to high priest. This turban-passing will continue until the Messiah arrives to take His place as God's final and ultimate Great High Priest.

There will be something different about Him, however. He won't come from the family of Levi, as Aaron did. Instead, Hebrews 7:17 says He's of the order of Melchizedek and His term of office will have no end.

In John 17:3, Jesus identifies Himself as this promised Christ. Though He's always our Great High Priest, Jesus shares His priestly duties with those who follow Him. As though passing his turban to them, Jesus turns to His disciples in John 20:21–22 and says, "As the Father has sent Me, I also send you." The crowning tiara of help comes when He breathes His Holy Spirit on them.

Like Aaron and his sons, we can feel a great weight of responsibilities on our heads when we follow God's call. The dreams He puts in our hearts can seem overwhelming to accomplish at times. Yet, He crowns us with His Holy Spirit to strengthen our resolve and maintain our dedication. With His help, we will always be "Holy to the LORD."

Fear not, for I am with you; be not dismayed, for I am your God. I will strengthen you, yes, I will help you (Isaiah 41:10).

Prayer: Holy Spirit, thank You for the promise of Your help as I run the race You've set before me. Strengthen my resolve to stay dedicated to You through every struggle along the way.

Deeper Still

Read Isaiah 41:8–13.

Whenever I doubt my capacity to finish what God has begun in me, I read these strong promises of help. Which of these verses bolsters your courage the most and why? Journal your thoughts.

Day 59

And It Was Good

Before we begin, read Exodus 39:32–43

Can you imagine being in the grand parade with the people bringing all they have made to Moses? We pile the utensils, the posts, the sockets, pins, and cords in heaps. We carry our jars of oil and containers of spices. Why, there's old Elisheba, bringing freshly baked bread for the table!

What an achievement. It hasn't been a full year since we left Egypt and the work's already completed. The air is thick with expectation—we're about to see the tent go up!

Before that can happen, however, all the work must be inspected. It should come as no surprise. God subjected His own handiwork to inspection as He created the universe. He examined it element by element, pronouncing each part "good" before moving on to the next.

Why not trust each artisan to judge his own work? The instructions, after all, are so precisely written, we can replicate the tabernacle today with a fair degree of accuracy. Unfortunately, some elements of the design aren't in the written record.

Several pieces of furniture, for example, are supposed to have "moldings of gold" around their rims, but their pattern isn't described. The lampstand surely has a base to stand it on, yet the design doesn't mention one. The ark's cherubim are described as having faces and wings, but what about their feet? Should they look like the hooves described in Ezekiel 1:7 or be more human-like?

Only someone who has actually seen the tabernacle in its finished form qualifies to judge the workmanship. Moses fits that bill because he saw the heavenly pattern in Exodus 25:9, when God met with him on the mountain.

Can you see him examining the pieces? He turns each board this way and that, weighing each silver socket, handling every clasp and hook, testing the weave of the curtains, and sniffing the spices. Can't you just hear communal sigh of relief when he declares the work approved? "Indeed they had done it; as the LORD had commanded" (Exodus 39:43).

Moses judges the workmanship of the tabernacle made of fabric, wood, and metal, but who can judge the dwelling place for God made of human beings — the body of Christ? Only someone who has been to heaven and seen the pattern. Having come from the Father and returned to Him again (John 16:28), Jesus walks through our pieces like Moses through the tabernacle. He doesn't measure us against one another, but against the pattern drawn for each of us by our Creator — the one who has designed a place for us in His heavenly tabernacle (Hebrews 8:1–2).

Wouldn't it be great if we left all judgment to Him? Unfortunately, we don't. We're made in God's image, so we share His ability to evaluate. We're supposed to use it to judge the plans in our hearts, the thoughts of our minds, and the labors of our hands against God's word. Instead, we often use it to measure ourselves or others against the pattern *we* think is right.

No wonder our evaluation often results with "disapproved," "inadequate," or "doesn't measure up" stamped to our foreheads. Only the one who's "been to the mountain" can be trusted to make that judgment—He's seen our pattern drawn with the finger of God in heaven. Let's trust Him to give us a true appraisal.

Therefore judge nothing before the time
(1 Corinthians 4:5).

Prayer: Lord Jesus, enable me to know Your evaluation of my condition. When the voice of others or even my own heart suggests a tweak to my design, enable me to see whether Your head is nodding in agreement.

Deeper Still

Read 1 Corinthians 4:1–5.
Paul talks about being careful not to even judge himself. What are some areas in which you've been hard on yourself lately? If you looked at yourself through the eyes of a parent, what would you want that child to know about those things? Journal your thoughts.

Day 60

We See in Part

Before we begin, read Exodus 39:32–43 again

We've brought our separate pieces to Moses. Now we await the "big reveal" of the tabernacle in full operation. What thoughts, do you think, might be racing around people's heads in this moment? Are the weavers speculating on what their curtains might finally cover? Do the makers of the bronze altar wonder what sacrifice could possibly be equal to it? Are the goldsmiths sighing just a bit as they turn their masterpieces over to Moses, knowing they'll never be allowed to touch, or even see, the holy articles again?

We've been working in hope. We've woven and carved and formed the pieces, but we can only understand the tabernacle through the part we've been working on. Trying to comprehend the whole, would make us like the proverbial blind men trying to make sense of an elephant.

Even today, we have *some* understanding of the piece God's put in our hand. We work in hope it will find its place as part of a fully functioning tabernacle. But capturing a vision of everything? All of us working together as smoothly as Moses' tabernacle did? That's a stretch.

It's hard for me to see the real value of my contribution without a clear picture of the whole. The only thing in my hand may be the little silver hook I've been working on. Next to someone's big curtain or shiny gold board, it seems inconsequential. What would it matter that if I cut corners in its production — if I skipped a small step in purifying its metal?

Well, what might have happened in the tabernacle if a few gold or bronze clasps hadn't come up to standards? The ceiling of the holy rooms might have been rent or given way. Weak pins or cords would have put the courtyard fence at risk of collapse.

The tabernacle relies on the smaller pieces as much as the larger ones. Allowing impurities to remain in my silver means the hooks I form might not be able to bear the weight of the great curtains they're meant to hold. I strive to be, as 2 Timothy 2:15 puts it, "approved to God, a worker who does not need to be ashamed" precisely *because* I'm not in a position to know the full consequences of my work. I see only in part and can't understand who might be affected by my contribution or whose life might rely on the quality of work I've done.

Our place in the tabernacle is more than who we are, it's what we're a part of. My victories in undergoing trials are not for my benefit alone, but for those who need to be supported by the strength I've gain through them.

Let's take our work seriously and produce a contribution of excellence for God's tabernacle. We don't yet know what great weight might hang on our little gift.

> *He who is faithful in what is least is faithful also*
> *in much; and he who is unjust in what is least*
> *is unjust also in much*
> *(Luke 16:10).*

Prayer: Father, help me take the work You've placed in my hands seriously. Give me eyes to see all the resources You've put within my reach to help me. Let me do my part with increasing excellence so the finished product brings honor to Your name.

Deeper Still

Read Matthew 25:14–30.
What are some of the talents has God given you? What are you doing (or what could you do) to invest in those gifts and help them grow? Journal your thoughts.

Week Six

Discussion Questions

This week we examined the giving nature of the linen garments, looked for the Holy Spirit's help in staying true to the Lord, considered the need to let Jesus be the final judge of our condition, and reminded ourselves we only see in part. Choose one or more of the following questions to consider on your own or discuss as a group.

1. What have you had to give up in order to benefit someone else? Did you lay it aside willingly or out of a sense of duty? What difference does love make in that process?
2. Can you describe an incident when the Holy Spirit's help was key to your staying true to the Lord?
3. Do you tend to judge yourself too harshly? Share suggestions with each other on how to let the Lord be your judge.
4. When was the last time you had trouble understanding your situation because you could only see part of the elephant mentioned in the devotion for Day 60? How might you encourage yourself in a current perplexing situation?
5. Questions? Insights? Look for "A Place for Me in God's Tent" on Facebook and join the conversation.

Part Three

The Place and He

Beginning in Exodus 40, Scripture describes the tabernacle in detail for the third time. All the components have been completed and Moses is at last ready to assemble the tent and initiate ministry operations. In this final set of devotions, we'll consider how Jesus is displayed as the fulfillment of all the tabernacle parts and functions. He is the ultimate dwelling place, not only for the Holy Spirit, but for us.

Week One

Day 61

Assembly Begins

Before we begin, read Exodus 40:2, 34–35

With this passage, the work of the earthly tabernacle enters a new phase. "On the first day of the first month" of Israel's second year out of Egypt, Moses begins to assemble all its parts.

So far, we've looked at the tabernacle design as it applies to us — whether as individual dwelling places for the Holy Spirit or as part of the many-membered body of believers Christ promises to inhabit (Matthew 18:20).

Today we begin considering what the tent design says about Messiah as God's sheltering tabernacle. How is Jesus foreshadowed as the coming Christ in all its parts, furnishings and ministries?

As soon as Moses approves its components and gets it assembled, a cloud covers the tabernacle, the glory of the Lord fills it, and the tabernacle begins fulfilling its destiny. Jesus begins His own ministry in a remarkably similar way. In Matthew 3:17, God the Father announces His approval as Jesus rises from the waters of the Jordan. "This is My beloved Son, in whom I am well pleased." The Holy Spirit falls upon Him — not as a cloud, but in the form of a dove. Approved by the Father and filled with the Holy Spirit, Jesus steps into His destiny.

We've already encountered Jesus as our High Priest in previous devotions, so we won't be surprised to discover more about Him in that role as we continue. But we'll also see Him throughout the tabernacle. He'll be in the firm support of the gold walls of the sanctuary, in the protective coverings of badger skins and leather, in the ark of the covenant and the table and the lamp. We'll watch Him minister at the altar of incense and slay the sacrifices at the bronze altar. He'll not only *bring* the offerings, He'll *be* the offerings as well.

It will be an awe-inspiring trip, but as we proceed, remember we are still part of this picture. We're still the stones on the breast and shoulders our Great High Priest as He enters the tabernacle. We are the lives in the silver sockets at His feet and we join the great cloud of witnesses in the milling crowds.

The promise of the tabernacle in full operation begins with today's reading. Hold your breath. We're about to watch the greatest acts of love ever performed on the earth.

For You have been a shelter for me, a strong tower
from the enemy. I will abide in Your tabernacle forever;
I will trust in the shelter of Your wings
(Psalm 61:3–4).

Prayer: Lord, open my eyes to see and understand the pattern in Your tabernacle.

Deeper Still

Read Hebrews 9:1–5.
From what you've learned already about these components of the tabernacle, in what ways can you already identify Jesus in them? Journal your thoughts.

Day 62

A Noisy Sheepfold

Before we begin, read Exodus 40:1-2

The first two times we encountered the tabernacle descriptions, they were loaded with details. This time, all God has Moses do is "set up the tabernacle of the tent of meeting." Because He doesn't mention its constituent parts here, the tent seems to appear on the first day as already complete.

It makes me think of John 1:1-3. "In the beginning was the Word, and the Word was with God, and the Word was God. He was in the beginning with God. All things were made through Him, and without Him nothing was made that was made." Though Jesus had to be born and develop as a human being, in some ways He was already fully formed and complete when He arrived as the Word of God.

We might consider Exodus 40:1-2 in the same light. In the beginning, was the tabernacle. The tabernacle *was* Christ, and Christ was *in* the tabernacle. Every part of the tabernacle that was made was made with Christ in mind, and without Him nothing in the tabernacle means anything at all.

Even the dimensions of the dwelling place speak of its designer. We know from Exodus 27, 36, and 38 that the courtyard is fifty cubits by one hundred, the inner tent thirty cubits by ten, and the Holy of Holies ten cubits in all three directions.

All these multiples of ten suggest something of perfection and completeness. God's perfect law, for example, is expressed in His ten holy commandments. Complete vindication for Israel was meted out with ten plagues of judgment against Egypt. Even today, we label something as "a perfect ten" to indicate it's as good as it gets.

Meanwhile, the multiple references to the number three in the inner tent (ten cubits times three for its length and ten cubits cubed for the Holy of Holies) hints at the three-fold nature of God — Father, Son and Holy Spirit.

We might say, then, that the tabernacle is a completely perfect dwelling place for a completely perfect God. And into this incredible habitation He has invited . . . us!

Now, why sully a flawless house with the muddy footprints of human beings? Maybe for the same reason God didn't stop after the fifth day of creation. The world was pretty much finished on day five, just as the tent is in Exodus 40. The only problem with either of these dwelling places was their emptiness. God wants a full house — one with sons and daughters filling its rooms with the noise of love and fellowship.

So, in the beginning was God, whose massive heart needed recipients for His great love. He was a dwelling place looking for a family, a shelter in search of someone to protect, a refuge longing to house weary travelers, an empty house yearning to be a home.

He has invited us to live in His house and be part of His family. Don't be afraid of stepping inside. He's already taken care of everything that might disqualify our presence. Come forward with confidence. His perfect dwelling place is ready to make us feel perfectly at home.

*I will put them together like sheep of the fold, like a
flock in the midst of their pasture; they shall make
a loud noise because of so many people
(Micah 2:12).*

Prayer: Father God, remind me how strongly You desire
to have Your house full when I'm discouraged about the
mud I drag into Your presence. Let me feel the depths of
Your desire to have me as part of Your family, as I wipe
my feet again and again at Your door.

Deeper Still

Read Luke 14:16–24.
Can you hear the desire in the voice of the householder in
this passage? Nothing would have been worse to him
than empty places at the table. Are there times you feel
you've ignored His invitation to break bread? What holds
you back from pulling up a chair with Him now? Journal
your thoughts.

Day 63

What Is It Worth

Before we begin, read Exodus 40:17–18

Yesterday, we thought about the tabernacle symbolically appearing as a completed place. In reality, it did have to be set up. Today, let's jump forward in Exodus to watch Moses assemble it.

The first order of business is setting the silver sockets in place, as well as the four pillars at the threshold to the Holy of Holies.

All this silver, you'll remember, came from the people's half-shekel contributions during the census (see "Silver Sockets, Silver Shekels" from Day 37 if you need to review).

A half-shekel, apparently, was a modest coin, so the required contribution was within everyone's grasp. Today it would be worth a little over three dollars. To be counted as one of God's people, the Israelites only needed to agree to the price God set and bring it to Him.

They could not, however, contribute just any silver coin in exchange for their lives. It had to meet the standards of the "tabernacle shekel." Its weight was precisely determined in Exodus 30:13. Should they present a counterfeit coin of mixed metals they'd be turned away at the tabernacle scales.

Like the Israelites of old, we can't redeem our lives with anything. Should we offer our own lives for our sins, our quality would be weighed and found wanting. One mistake, one blemish on our record, and our coinage would be rejected.

Henry W. Soltau put it this way: "[God] has one standard of perfection and purity, against which He weighs the hearts, spirits, and actions of men (Soltau 1972, 86)." That standard is His Messiah. Jesus alone fulfills all God's requirements of righteousness. His life is as pure and acceptable as the tabernacle shekel. If we want to be counted as part of God's family, it's His life we must present as our redemption.

Our part in this process is so modest. The life which cost Jesus everything to give costs many of us little more than our pride to receive. Nevertheless, that little bow of the knee can be extraordinarily difficult.

You'd think He'd be annoyed we contribute so little to our own salvation, but Hebrews 12:2 says it was His joy to take on our whole debt with His life.

In fact, I can picture Him now in the heavenly tabernacle, His feet surrounded by the massive silver sockets. Every gram represents a life He bought back from death. I can hear the triumph in His voice as He points to the shining baseboard and trumpets to His Father. "Here am I and the children whom the LORD has given me!" (Isaiah 8:18). "Of those whom You gave Me I have lost none" (John 18:9).

"If you confess with your mouth the Lord Jesus and believe in your heart that God has raised Him from the dead, you will be saved" (Romans 10:9).

Prayer: Lord Jesus, who am I that You would pay such a price to add my name to Your book? May I ever give You thanks by living this life You've purchased in ways that please You.

Deeper Still

Read 1 Peter 1:17–21.

Imagine the difference between the value of a coin (no matter how pure) and the value of Christ's perfect life. Now imagine the difference between confessing what He's done for you and the price He paid to do it. What thanksgiving can you bring Him today? Journal your thoughts.

Day 64

A Mediator Who Knows Us Both

Before we begin, read Exodus 40:17–18 again

Moses is snapping gold-wrapped boards of acacia wood into the sockets. Hand-like projections between the boards lock them together. Through the boards' rings, He slides wood and gold poles, stabilizing them as walls. To finish the tabernacle's skeleton, Moses sets four pillars (made of acacia overlaid in gold) into the sockets, forming the threshold into the Holy of Holies where the veil will hang.

The entire support structure of the inner rooms is made of wood and gold married together. It reverberates with the messages of Emmanuel — a Messiah with us who is both God and man.

There's a permanence implied in this dual nature. The wood and gold of the tabernacle, after all, would never be pulled apart. As many times as the Israelites tore down the tabernacle, they'd always be one, just as Messiah would forever be both Son of Man and Son of God.

The humanity of Christ's "wood" qualifies Him as a substitute for man. He needs to take on a body capable of dying or He can't die *as* a human *for* humans. Messiah's flesh also puts Him in touch with the needs, desires, and condition of His brethren. He knows the stress of resisting temptation, the pain of loss and betrayal, the frustration of being misunderstood, and the tension between pleasing God and pleasing people. He understands what drives the human heart to heights of joy and courage, what impels it to endure, and what empowers it to love.

At the same time, the divinity of His "gold" gives Jesus a distinctive ability to relate to the Father, to know the stresses, pain, disappointments, frustrations, joys, and excitement inherent in being Judge of all the earth.

In other words, Christ not only knows the ups and downs of being human, He knows the challenges and thrills of being God. What better mediator to stand between us, to put one hand on God's shoulder and the other on ours? What better High Priest to serve God and advocate for human beings?

> *For we do not have a High Priest who cannot*
> *sympathize with our weaknesses, but was in*
> *all points tempted as we are, yet without sin*
> *(Hebrews 4:15).*

Prayer: Jesus, I'm so glad You know what it's like to be in my skin. Help me to also trust what You know about the Father's needs and desires in every situation. Help me be patient as You reconcile my needs with those of the Father's.

Deeper Still

Read Hebrews 2:14–3:6.
How does the first part of this reading help you see Christ as someone who understands what it's like to be you? Which of His responsibilities as God's Son (mentioned in the last part of this reading) might He have

to consider while He's ministering to you? Journal your thoughts.

Day 65

Love in Four Layers

Before we begin, read Exodus 40:19

We already looked in detail at the four layers that covered the tabernacle (the linen curtains, the goat hair curtains, the ram skins dyed red, and the badger skins). Together, they produce a stunning foreshadow of the Messiah.

The finest, most beautiful layer drops over the frame first. The linen curtains with their fine-twined fibers testify to a pure and righteousness nature. The scarlet, blue, and purple threads weave a story of bloody sacrifice, an origin from heaven, and a destiny as King. The cherubim flying throughout the embroidery suggest a divine army, on alert to give Him aid and support.

Over it all drops the goat hair curtains. Dark and somber as a mourner's cloak, this layer buries the beauty of the linen under the fabric of goats — animals given a dreadful destiny in the New Testament (Matthew 25:31–46). This set of curtains contains a disturbing number of panels — eleven. As a number, it heralds neither the perfection of ten nor the governmental order of twelve. Instead, it carries a sense of disorder and unbalance. Kevin J. Connor, in *The Tabernacle of Moses*, suggests the number even implies lawlessness. (Conner 1976, 63)

Why would God cover a symbol of righteousness with one of wickedness and sin? Because Messiah is destined to carry the sins of many on His back (1 Peter 2:24).

Fortunately, darkness and foreboding does not have the last word. Moses hurls the red ram's skins over it next, drowning the black under a sea of red. No measurements limit the dyed leather's coverage, and neither would Christ's blood be poured out in measure. It would suffice to thoroughly cover sin.

We've already seen the harsh history of the ram skins (See "Skins and Leather" on Day 12). Stripped from their owner, they were brined in putrid tanning chemicals before being soaked in dye. Their story would only hint at the indignities Jesus would suffer, before His blood poured out to cover us all. "Surely He has borne our griefs and carried our sorrows. . . . He was wounded for our transgressions, He was bruised for our iniquities; the chastisement for our peace was upon Him, and by His stripes we are healed" (Isaiah 53:4–5).

One layer remains to cover the tent—the mysterious badger skins. In one sense, they reflect Messiah's lack of "form or comeliness" mentioned in Isaiah 53:2. In another way, they remind me of a different use for these skins suggested in Scripture—shoe leather (Ezekiel 16:10).

The idea of sandal fabric being tossed over everything brings my thoughts to Ruth 4:7. "Now this was the custom in former times in Israel concerning redeeming and exchanging, to confirm anything: one man took off his sandal and gave it to the other, and this was a confirmation in Israel."

To me, the addition of this final covering is like God casting His shoe over the tabernacle—claiming the people who shelter under His wings as His own.

In the four layers of the tent and its coverings, we see the scope of Messiah's nature and mission. He is perfect in righteousness, yet carries the sin of the world on His back. Torn and broken in the flesh, His blood has poured, in endless supply, to completely cover sin and pay for all unrighteousness. Over it all, God throws His shoe—announcing to all He will care for us as His own.

*But now, thus says the LORD, who created you,
O Jacob, and He who formed you, O Israel: "Fear not,
for I have redeemed you; I have called you by your
name; you are Mine"
(Isaiah 43:1).*

Prayer: Father, Your love leaves me in awe. Who am I that You would want me so much—that You would pay such a price to call me Your own? May I never doubt Your devotion to me. May I never let go of my devotion to You.

Deeper Still

Read Ezekiel 16:4–14.

As you read this passage, think of yourself as the person being washed. Imagine God dropping His red leather over your goat hair curtains. As you read about the woman being clothed in linen and silk, picture yourself being dressed with the beautiful inner curtains. As the author's wings spread out, see God spread His badger skin over you and call you His own. Journal your thoughts.

Week One

Discussion Questions

This week we began thinking about the tabernacle as representing Christ Himself. We marveled at God's welcome for us as imperfect guests in His perfect home and noticed Jesus alone measured up to the "tabernacle shekel." We saw Jesus in the wood and gold of the tabernacle furniture—in His dual human and divine nature. Choose one or more of the following questions to consider on your own or discuss as a group.

1. Why do you think God puts up with imperfect humans running around His perfect home? Can you relate to His feelings about you as either a parent or a child yourself?
2. As you think of the wood and gold combination in the tabernacle as representing Christ, what is the value you find in the human part of His nature? How does it matter to you that He also carries the gold of divinity?
3. Everyone's cost in bending the knee to Jesus is a bit different. Some give up only their pride. Are there some circumstances in your life that makes your cost to say yes to Christ's invitation especially high? Take a moment to pray for one another as you each pay the price required to follow Him.

4. Questions? Insights? Look for "A Place for Me in God's Tent" on Facebook and join the conversation.

Week Two

Day 66

The Heart of God

Before we begin, read Exodus 25:10–16, 37:1–5, and 40:20

We looked briefly at the ark in "A Box of Memories" on Day 42. Let's go back for a bit to consider the details in a different light.

The ark was the first piece of the tabernacle God described to Moses in Exodus 25. It was the first item of furniture Bezalel addressed in Exodus 37. In Exodus 40, it is first to take its place in the heart of the tent.

It's a fitting spot for an object so beautifully descriptive of the heart of God. Its deceptively simple design proclaims an astonishingly complex picture not only of God, but also of Christ in His fullness.

The frame is made from the wood of the acacia — a tree whose canopy is crowned with thorns and whose hard, dense wood suggests indestructibility. It is covered inside and out with gold and finished around its top with a crown-like molding. Together these details hint at a Messiah who would be empowered by an incorruptible life, humbled under a crown of thorns, and rise with a crown of glory.

As we noticed before, the finished ark will hold three items — the Ten Commandments, Aaron's budded rod, and a sample of the manna God provided in the wilderness.

What a picture of God's persona. Commandments etched in stone proclaim the unchangeable character of His words and His role as Lawgiver. The shielding mercy seat demonstrates His protective nature. The staff of Aaron identifies Him as the source of all authority, whose Messiah would be Shepherd to His people and Lord of all His heavenly hosts. The miraculous nature of the sprouted rod precedes Jesus' announcement in John 11:25 that He is the resurrection and the life. The sample of manna foreshadows His role as the bread of life and miracle-worker (John 6:48–51).

Though some of Christ's nature can be seen in the holy place and the courtyard (we find forgiveness at His altar, nourishment at His table, wisdom from His lampstand, make petitions at His altar of incense), nothing speaks as clearly about His nature as the ark in the Holy of Holies. To know Him this intimately, we must meet Him behind the veil.

The problem is, Exodus 33:20 says no one can see God and live — not without protection anyway. Before the tabernacle went up, Moses found protection in the cleft of the rock in Exodus 33:18–23, where he hid as the Lord passed by. Later, the tent design itself would provide many protections (the blood on the brazen altar, the door of the holy place, the veil of the Holy of Holies, and the mercy seat over the ark).

We no longer need to find a rocky crevice to hide in or a singular earthly tent to act as our refuge if we want to draw near to God. Every protection we need is in the person after whom the tabernacle was designed — the Son of God, Jesus the Christ.

He *is* the altar, the door, the veil, the mercy seat that make an intimate relationship with God possible. Come close. Draw near. There are mysteries about God, which can only be unraveled for you in the light of His presence.

Come to the ark and let Jesus introduce you to the Father you never knew.

Call to Me, and I will answer you, and show you
great and mighty things, which you do not know
(Jeremiah 33:3).

Prayer: Jesus, introduce me to the Father You know. Help me fall in love with Him and see Him as You do.

Deeper Still

Read 2 Corinthians 3:12–18.

There's a great parallel made between Moses and us in this passage. Like Moses, we can't help but carry something of the Lord away with us after being near Him. Have you ever had to "hide" some of the splendor you experienced after being with Him? How have you handled that? Journal your thoughts.

Day 67

The Ark Gets a Lid

Before we begin, read Exodus 25:17–22, 37:6–9, and 40:20

We know that the tablets Moses brought down from the mountain rest in the ark. As temples of the Holy Spirit, we keep God's words in our hearts in much the same way the tabernacle cradles the Ten Commandments in its ark. The "house rules" they describe are good. They promise comfort, order, and benefits if they're followed. If they're violated, however, these otherwise good laws pronounce harsh punishments ranging from separation to outright death for the guilty.

Our Host badly wants to fill His tent with family, but He has no illusions about our ability to stick to His rules. He had a choice to make, when He first drew up the tabernacle plans, in order to make it possible for us to live with Him. He could destroy or modify the laws He already had in place, in order to make them easier for us to follow. That made no sense, however, because He'd already determined they were absolutely just and right. His other option was to find a way to protect the ones He loves from the consequences of our inevitable disobedience. His solution? Give the ark a lid.

As we've seen, most of the tent furniture either contains elements of wood or takes on the appearance of wood, reflecting a connection between God and man. The ark itself, framed in acacia and wrapped in gold, echoes the theme. When it comes to the ark's lid, however, nothing but pure gold will do. No human influence mars the device that will separate man from the full force of the law inside the ark. This is a boundary fixed by God alone.

The hammered gold cover is called the Mercy Seat. With its flat central portion flanked by two cherubim rising like arm rests, it does indeed resemble a seat—a throne from which God will meet His people face-to-face. Splashed upon it once a year, sacrificial blood will touch its surface. Its presence will testify that a life has been given for a life upon the brazen altar and justice has been satisfied. It likewise satisfies God's need for mercy, because it means frail mankind has gone free.

An Old Testament prophet would cry out to God in Habakkuk 3:2, "In wrath remember mercy." The fact was, God had already answered his plea in the tabernacle. Psalm 85:10 would describe the place where the box with the law met the lid with the blood. "Mercy and truth have met together; righteousness and peace have kissed."

God's good news isn't that He's stopped considering the law. It isn't that He's closing His eyes and no longer applying it. It's that He has made a shield between us and the judgment we so richly deserve.

The golden lid of the ark—God's landing place for mercy.

You have forgiven the iniquity of Your people; You have covered all their sin (Psalm 85:2).

Prayer: Jesus, how can I thank You for standing between me and the punishment I have earned for myself? Thank You for being the shield that covers me so I can continue to dwell in Your house forever.

Deeper Still

Read Psalm 85.

The psalmist both rejoices about the times God turned His wrath away and pleads with Him to do so again. Have you been confident of God's mercy one minute and worried it may no longer be available in the next? How does the firmness of the mercy seat settle your heart to believe He will extend His mercy to you as readily today as He did in the past? Journal your thoughts.

Day 68

Hiding no More

Before we begin, read Exodus 40:21

The ark and veil seem to share an air of secrecy.

Once the ark is safely inside the Holy of Holies, no one but the high priest would ever see it again (with a couple of deadly exceptions). Even on the one day of the year he was allowed to peek behind the veil, the high priest would catch little more than a glimpse. When he pulls the curtain aside, the smoke of incense will rush in to obscure it.

Nevertheless, the tabernacle and all its components would have to be moved whenever God gave the order. For those times, the priests would take the veil down and use it to cover the ark. Before bringing it out of the tabernacle, the veil itself would be hidden by the badger skins and a blue cloth. (You can find the whole process of disassembling the tabernacle and prepping it for travel in Numbers 4, if you want to read more).

Why all this hiding? Perhaps because the people weren't yet prepared to survive an unfiltered encounter with God.

Their first experience with God's presence hadn't gone well. One look at Mount Sinai exploding with lightning and smoke, one explosion of thunder, and the people were ready to run. "You speak with us, and we will hear," they told Moses in Exodus 20:19, shoving him forward, "but let not God speak with us, lest we die." Even though Moses went to talk with God for them, the people were terrified to see even the residual shine on his face (Exodus 34:29–30).

Approaching God can be a harrowing experience. After all, "God is light and in Him is no darkness at all" (1 John 1:5). In this light, every blot and stain on our conscience stands out like red wine on a white dress. Every clever reasoning that seemed justified in our own minds is shown for the lame excuse that it is. No argument remains against His Word in the glare of this light. We stand condemned, unless we know with absolute certainty that we won't be counted "guilty as charged."

As long as we're tormented by the fear of being punished, we need the screen. We're *grateful* for it. It gives us an excuse to stay outside the Holy of Holies.

But God didn't build the tabernacle to keep us at arm's length. He set it up so His children could draw near Him.

What could God do about it? His people were afraid He was going to punish them. If only He could convince them of His love, it would cast away their fear (1 John 4:18). To help them grasp the tremendous depth and extent of His love for them, He set in motion a solution that would open the veil—God would come out of hiding.

He'd send His Son Jesus to the altar as a sacrificial lamb. His life would be such a perfect offering, it would count as the people's burnt, sin, peace, grain, and trespass offerings all rolled into one. His death would assure forgiveness, guarantee mercy, and prove God's love.

As Jesus' final breath leaves His body, God takes hold of the top of the veil and rips it apart all the way to the ground. In Matthew 27:51, God's love breaks out and presses toward mankind. He will wait no longer to touch His children. He will wait no more to quiet their fears.

The veil is taken away in Christ
(2 Corinthians 3:14).

Prayer: Lord Jesus, forgive me for allowing fear to separate me from You. Your love has paid the price to guarantee mercy. Help me take an ever-bolder step toward You now.

Deeper Still

Read Matthew 26:26–29.

As you see Jesus tear the bread apart, imagine the veil splitting open. What frightens you most about getting closer to God? As He tears the bread, see Him rip that fear in two. Journal your thoughts.

Day 69

The Next Act Opens

Before we begin, read Exodus 40:21 again

Last time, we noted the veil would one day no longer stand between worshippers and God. It won't happen until long after the tabernacle is replaced with the temple, but let's pretend for a moment it happens in Moses' days. What might it be like to serve in the tabernacle just as Jesus dies on the cross?

We stop by the laver to wash after entering through the gate. At the bronze altar we present our offering, then push aside the door to the tabernacle and slip into the holy place. Our eyes blink a moment as they adjust to the change in lighting. Even in the subdued lamplight, the gold furniture and walls bedazzle us. Stepping up to the altar of incense, we take in the elaborate veil before us. Giant cherubim, dressed in bold colors, gaze at us from the wall-sized tapestry. For a moment, we think we're confronting the two fiery guardians standing before the garden of Eden

A censer filled with incense is in our hand. As we prepare to sprinkle it onto the coals before us, the earth begins to rumble. Then it bucks like a mustang resisting a saddle, and we almost lose our footing. From above, we hear the plink of snapping threads—slowly at first, then faster, faster. The noise of ripping fabric escalates in pitch and volume like the sound of a great cat screeching. The hair on the back of our necks stands at attention until the final bit of curtain snaps apart at our feet and the ground stills.

We hold our breath. Bits of lint float in the air, dusty in the lamplight. Slow and shallow, we inhale . . . then straighten up.

The veil hangs in two, its halves sagging left and right like stage curtains pulled open. Its woven cherubim have likewise stepped aside. A beam of light from the lampstand beside us illuminates the once darkened Holy of Holies, shining like a spotlight on the golden ark. Two different cherubim are before us now, but they aren't facing us. Their attention is on the space between them, where the lead character now takes up center stage — the fiery cloud of Almighty God.

The God who was hidden now stands face-to-face with us. All the complaints we brought with us to present at His altar, all the questions we thought about asking, drop to the dust of the tabernacle floor. "Prepare yourself," His voice thunders as it did in Job 40:7, "and I will question you, and you shall answer Me."

We have no answer and we know it. But our hands still hold a second bowl, filled with the blood of the sacrificial lamb we brought from the brazen altar. Trembling, we stretch it forward. "Consider the substitute, Lord, and have mercy," we say.

The fiery cloud transforms. Hot fear melts into warm welcome. Smiling eyes take shape in the smoke and hands reach out from the haze to take our cup. "It is enough," He says and pours it at His feet. His eyes seem to penetrate us, yet His voice is tender, soft as a breeze. "Enter into the joy of your Father. Judgment is over. You need fear it no more."

I have heard of You by the hearing of the ear,
but now my eye sees You
(Job 42:5).

Prayer: Heavenly Father, when I consider Your heavens, the work of Your fingers, the moon and the stars, which You have ordained, who am I that You care about me?

Deeper Still

Have you considered what an honor it is to be welcomed into the presence of God? Take a moment to pray Psalm 145 to the Lord. Journal your thoughts.

Day 70

Tested and True

Before we begin, read Exodus 40:22–23

We've survived our visit to the face of God at the ark and lived! We no longer fear judgment is hanging over our heads like the sword of Damocles. It's a good time to bring the table in (honestly, who could have thought about eating without knowing for sure we were welcome?).

The purpose of a table is to present something satisfying to those who gather around it. Daniel R. Hyde says in his book *God in our Midst*, "By placing the twelve loaves on the table, the priest symbolically offered up the people to the Lord, and they were accepted as a sweet-smelling offering to Him." (Hyde 2012, 74)

Once God is satisfied with the bread in His presence, He will focus on satisfying His people. Leviticus 24:8–9 shows how He'd do that. Acting as any head of a household might, God shares His food with the others at the table. The only problem with the picture of bread on the table is, by the time the priests get to bite into it, the loaves will have already been sitting on the table for a whole week. Now, when was the last time you left bread out that long and still found it edible? Yet, like the manna that never spoiled inside the ark, there's apparently a miraculous freshness to these loaves.

With the loaves stacked tightly together within the table's rim, they take on the aspect of a single, enormous loaf made of many parts. Compacted together, they form another type of picture of the Messiah—the single body made of many members who, in this case, is represented as the Bread of Life.

Bread is associated with God's words several places in Scripture. Deuteronomy 8:3 says, for example, "Man does not live on bread alone but on every word that comes from the mouth of the LORD" (NIV). The table then, at least in part, speaks to us of feeding on words coming from God.

There are plenty of words available for consumption in this world, but they don't all qualify as good food for us. What tastes sweet in our mouths and goes sour in our stomachs won't, in the end, nourish us.

When God speaks, He doesn't carelessly fling words around just because they sound good. Psalm 12:6 says He tests them first. "The words of the LORD are pure words, like silver tried in a furnace of earth, purified seven times." The bread sitting on the table for seven days seems to reflect this sense of tested truth. Only after God keeps it under His sovereign eye for a week, is it ready for the priest to break it into separate pieces and share it as food.

Jesus is described as the Word of God in John 1:1 and calls Himself the Bread of Life in John 6:35. As the heavenly model for the earthly table of showbread, He is the wisdom of God lived out loud in a human being. Tested and true, He is God's Word transformed into human flesh. The story we read in His life gives us a more rounded understanding of what God is trying to explain to us in Scripture.

If you struggle with Old Testament teachings, try looking for ways Jesus lived them out. His actions add dimension to our understanding and turn the dry flour of Scripture into bread full of flavor.

I am the bread of life. He who comes to Me shall never hunger (John 6:35).

Prayer: Jesus, help me keep a picture of You in my mind whenever I read God's Word. Show me how You understand His will so that I can understand it too.

Deeper Still

Read John 6:43–51.

Jesus seems to hint that, though the manna pointed to Him, it was different from Him. How would you compare the bread of manna to the bread of life? Journal your thoughts.

Week Two

Discussion Questions

This week we saw the tabernacle display Christ as Lawgiver, Shepherd, and Resurrection in the ark. We discussed how God sometimes seems to hide from us and watched His joy at coming out of hiding. Finally, we saw how trustworthy the wisdom of God is. Choose one or more of the following questions to consider on your own or discuss as a group.

1. Have you ever been afraid to approach God? Is there anything about the tabernacle design that reassures you about your welcome?
2. What do you think it would have been like to be in the temple the day the veil split apart? Have you ever had a similarly powerful experience with God you'd be willing to share with the group?
3. Talk about the difference between trusting God's words and those that come from wise-sounding human intelligence. Can you describe a situation where you responded to the wrong wisdom?
4. Questions? Insights? Look for "A Place for Me in God's Tent" on Facebook and join the conversation.

Week Three

Day 71

Take Your Time at the Table

Before we begin, read Exodus 40:22–23 again

Absorbing the full benefit of a meal requires more than consumption. It needs digestion.

With natural food, we begin by experiencing the taste and smell and feel of food in our mouths by chewing. If we decide to swallow, the food moves on to our stomach and beyond. Then digestion really takes off. Bit by bit, the food is broken into ever-smaller pieces until it's tiny enough to pass into our bloodstream. It travels to every part of our body, nourishing and eventually becoming part of us.

It's much the same with spiritual food. We taste by reading or listening to Scripture. After chewing a bit, we decide whether we will swallow it (believe it) or not. The more time we give the Word of God to remain in our system by pondering and considering it, the more fully digested it becomes. The more it's digested, the more it becomes part of who we are.

Works like a charm — as long as things taste good.

It's easy to consume the Bible passages that are sweet as honey in our mouths. The less palatable passages are harder to swallow and even more difficult to digest. We sometimes want to spit them out entirely.

In the spirit, as in the natural, what we *like* to eat and what we *need* to eat are sometimes two different things. If I expect my food to nourish me, I may sometimes have to swallow what doesn't make my mouth happy.

When I first started reading the Bible, I found much of it unsavory and indigestible. Huge swaths of Scripture perplexed me completely. Why in the world, I wondered, is the book of Job included in the Bible? And for heaven's sake, what was I supposed to do with Revelation? Or Numbers? Or Leviticus?

On top of that, bad news seemed to bump into me every time I read it. Much of what I was doing seemed to be wrong, but I had no power to change it. So I opted for avoidance. I just wouldn't "eat" what I didn't like. Eventually, I stopped bothering to open my Bible at all.

Fortunately, my desire for God finally outweighed my dread and I decided to try reading it again. "Look, God, I'm going to read this, but I'm not promising to do anything about it." (I thought lightning might strike for that bit of insolence, but it didn't.)

So I read — what I liked and what I didn't. When I got to the end, I started over and read again. And again. Each time, the indigestible parts seemed to soften a bit. Eventually, the verses in one part of the Bible began to resonate with passages elsewhere. Over time, my spiritual taste buds even seemed to change. I began savoring what I'd never enjoyed before and God's word became real food to me.

No one is going to make sense of the whole Bible at first go-round. Digestion takes time and so does understanding. What we refuse to take in will never nourish us, so let's hold the Bread of Life in our hearts and minds a bit longer. Let's not be in a rush to get up from His table.

But he who received seed on the good ground is he who hears the word and understands it, who indeed bears fruit and produces: some a hundredfold, some sixty, some thirty (Matthew 13:23).

Prayer: Father God, help me give You the time You need to make your Word part of me. Help me hold it in my mouth long enough to allow You to soften it into nourishment for me.

Deeper Still

Read Matthew 13:3–23.

Jesus' final words in this parable describe the three processes required to absorb nutrition from God's Word. Hearing (eating), understanding (digesting) and bearing fruit (letting it become part of us). What happens when you try acting on Scriptures you haven't fully digested yet? How does it differ when you act on those that have become part of your heart and soul? Journal your thoughts.

Day 72

No Need of the Sun

Before we begin, read Exodus 40:24–25

When Moses set the table in place, the door to the holy place was still open. Sunlight allowed him to see what he was doing. Once the door is up, however, the room will go dark.

Without light, there can be no ministry in the tabernacle. There might be some bumping around in the dark, some knocking about of bread off the table, a bit of catching on fire of the priestly robes at the altar of incense, but no orderly worship will take place unless the priests can see.

God is sometimes described in Scriptures such as Psalm 97:2 as being clothed in "clouds and darkness." That would aptly describe the holy place except for the arrival of the shining lampstand.

Outside the tabernacle, natural illumination reveals many aspects of God. Creation itself is something of a self-portrait of its Maker. Psalm 19:1 says, "The heavens declare the glory of God; and the firmament shows His handiwork." The apostle Paul reminds us in Romans 1:20 that everything God made holds clues about who He is. "For since the creation of the world His invisible attributes are clearly seen, being understood by the things that are made."

Though we can understand something of God this way, human intelligence cannot illuminate the deep things of His heart any more than natural light can penetrate the inner rooms of the tabernacle. To really know God, we need a supernatural lamp.

The wisdom emanating from Christ's words, actions, and character, shines like the glittering light of the lampstand in the holy place. Everything about Jesus reveals aspects of God's character we can't see otherwise. Accepting Him as the lamp for our feet and the light to our path is like entering the holy place and seeing what would otherwise be out of view. He fills our hearts with a light that never goes out. As 1 John 1:5 says, "God is light and in Him is no darkness at all."

We have an advantage the priests of the Old Testament didn't have. For all but the high priest, the lampstand would only shed light in the holy place. For us, the veil has been pulled aside and Jesus' life now illuminates the Holy of Holies itself, revealing more about the Father, Son, and Holy Spirit than has ever been accessible before.

Let's take full advantage of this amazing gift and spend all the time we can in His light so He can show us great and mighty things we never knew before (Jeremiah 33:3).

For it is the God who commanded light to shine
out of darkness, who has shone in our hearts to give
the light of the knowledge of the glory of God in the
face of Jesus Christ
(2 Corinthians 4:6).

Prayer: Lord Jesus, thank you for shining a light on who God is. Show me something about Him I never knew before.

Deeper Still

Read 1 Corinthians 2:9–16.

Paul talks about things that can only be spiritually understood. What is one thing you understand about God now which you could never have understood before you accepted His invitation into His tent. Journal your thoughts.

Day 73

Timeless Power

Before we begin, read Exodus 40:24–25 again

We've looked at the lampstand several times now (in Days 8, 44, 45, and 72) and considered how its design foreshadows a Messiah who would be light to our darkness. John 1:4 speaks of Jesus by saying, "In Him was life, and the life was the light of men." Yet the lampstand has another tale to tell of the promised one—He is resurrection itself.

In all the descriptions of the menorah, nowhere has God described some kind of base to hold it. Metaphorically, the lampstand seems to represent a tree without roots, a branch cut off from the earth. If we look carefully at this seemingly dead tree, however, its buds and blossoms and fruit suggest it's somehow alive.

Now, normal trees produce buds, blossoms ,and fruit consecutively. The lampstand in the holy place, however, bears all three at once. Somehow this light-bearing branch, which was dead, but now lives, is beyond time.

When Jesus comes to the earth, He claims to be the light of the world in John 8:12, then adds in verse 58, "before Abraham was, I AM." Jesus, then, is unhindered by time. As part of the Godhead (Father, Son and Holy Spirit), He knows the end from the beginning. In

Revelation 1:8, Jesus appears to the apostle John and declares He not only was, but is, and is to come.

Our lives operate in a dramatic contrast. Situations for us are either in bud or in blossom or they're fully set with fruit. Hope buds in us with the promise of beauty yet to come. When its flower finally opens, we seem to revel in its charm for only a moment before the petals fall away and all seems dead again. Gradually, we discern that fruit has been swelling within us as imperceptibly as it does in earthly plants. Eventually, harvest comes.

We cycle through budding promise, emerging beauty, dying dreams and reborn fruitfulness. Each season seems either fleeting or endless, from our time-conscious perspective. The lampstand reminds us God is above time. He is at once in our present and our future, making sure all works out for our good.

What sustains the tabernacle's almond tree and enables its supernatural cycles is not its connection to the earth, but its supply of oil and fire — both used frequently as symbols of the Holy Spirit. While the source of oil is the same for all the lamps on the menorah, the side lamps are only lit by the flame on the central branch — and that fire is ignited by coals from the brazen altar.

When Jesus leaves His disciples in John 16:7–15, He tells them it is to their advantage He is going away. Until He dies on the cross, there would be no holy fire for their lamps. After He rises, He ignites them in Acts 2 with enough power to take three thousand souls from seedtime to harvest in a single day on Pentecost.

The supernatural oil and flame of the tabernacle lampstand is like the working of the Holy Spirit within us. He not only empowers us to survive cycles of life, death, and rebirth when they are tediously sequential. He also gives us hope God may override the natural order of events with miraculous ones, giving us bud and blossom and fruit all at once.

Let us go to Him in the holy place, day by day, and ask Him to replenish our oil and relight our flame.

Therefore being exalted to the right hand of God, and having received from the Father the promise of the Holy Spirit, He poured out this which you now see and hear
(Acts 2:33).

Prayer: Lord Jesus, keep reminding me You are beyond time. Fill me with the oil of Your Holy Spirit and ignite my spirit with Your fire until I produce a supernatural harvest for You.

Deeper Still

Read Acts 2.
Something in Peter's speech pierced his audience in their hearts. If you had been there that day, what would have impacted you most about what he said? Would it have frightened or excited you? Journal your thoughts.

Day 74

Help at the Altar of Incense

Before we begin, read Exodus 40:26–28

Once more, we stand at the altar of incense — a piece of furniture which will be separated from the ark by the veil alone. The smoldering coals on this altar aren't burning sacrifices but incense, raising a sweet and spicy cloud of smoke before our faces.

To keep the embers from going out, Aaron and his sons will have to attend the golden altar morning and evening, freshening the coals and adding more incense. At the heavenly counterpart of this altar, however, Romans 8:34 says Christ is always on duty. There, He pours out fresh incense of prayer before the Father as He pleads for us day and night.

Whenever we go to the place of prayer, whether at the height of noon or in the wee hours of night, we will find our Great High Priest already there. Romans 8:26 says the Holy Spirit will also be helping us at the altar. He'll be welling up from our heart's depth to direct and energize our prayers. More than that, Christ is not only present as Priest, but as the altar itself, supporting our incense-filled censer and holding it up before the Lord.

But that's not all. Revelation 8:3–4 paints a picture of an angel standing before the heavenly altar. He was "given much incense, that he should offer it with the prayers of all the saints."

With the prayers of the saints. Did you get that? We bring our prayers to the Father and pour them out on the altar of prayer, then Christ takes His own pile of incense and dumps it on top of ours. What a cloud of smoke must rise! Can you see it?

When my heart is heavy and my concerns desperate, when my faith seems inadequate to form the right words, what a comfort it is stepping beside someone already busy at the altar. How wonderful to have Him pour His perfect prayers over my feeble ones, turning my wispy plume into a column of smoke rising to heaven.

Reverend Canon Falloon described the scene beautifully in this quote from Frederick Whitfield's *The Tabernacle Priesthood and Offerings of Israel.*

> "Here we see Christ engaged in His work above; receiving the prayers of His people into His censer; taking their requests all into His own hand; making them His own; laying them on Himself as their golden altar; adding to them the savor of His own merits, so that they shall not go alone, unaccompanied or unwelcome, into His Father's presence; but . . . shall ascend up before God with a *certainty* of being heard and accepted there." (Whitfield 1884, 106–107)

Next time you go to prayer, remember Jesus is already there. Picture Him standing beside you at the altar of incense as your High Priest. Watch Him pour out the contents of His censer over your prayers on the coals. With His incense on top of yours, how could the smoke escape God's attention?

Likewise the Spirit also helps in our weaknesses. For we do not know what we should pray for as we ought, but the Spirit Himself makes intercession for us with groanings which cannot be uttered
(Romans 8:26).

Prayer: Lord Jesus, here I am with my little censer of incense. My faith in my own prayers is not great. Let Your Holy Spirit well up within in me and help me find words to express what's in my heart. Then pour Your incense over mine and carry the smoke of it to our Father.

Deeper Still

Read Psalm 20.

In the pronouncement of this blessing, can you see yourself as the recipient of remembered prayer? Which particular parts of this blessing resonate with you? Journal your thoughts.

Day 75

For Priests Alone

Before we begin, read Exodus 40:30–32

Moses is bringing in the fifth and final piece of tabernacle furniture. The laver is not the site of ministerial duties, per se. It's for a cleansing that is only available to the priests.

Were we to time-warp back to Moses' day, I doubt anyone reading this would qualify to wash there. We'd have to prove our lineage went back to Levi. This worked fine for the Israelites until the tabernacle gave way to the temple, and the temple was destroyed. After seventy years of exile in Babylon, the people were eager to go home and rebuild it. They returned to Israel only to find many of them could no longer verify their genealogy. Nehemiah 7:64 says those who couldn't prove they were from the line of Levi were excluded from the priesthood.

Since then, genealogical records have been lost or destroyed, making proof of tribal affiliation more and more problematic. If it was difficult for the Jews in Nehemiah's day to qualify for the priesthood, how can any of us living so much later claim the status of a priest in God's heavenly tabernacle?

One of the many Old Testament passages pointing to the coming Messiah is Psalm 110. It announces Him as "a priest forever according to the order of Melchizedek."

"First mentions" are always significant in Scripture. The very first mention of *anyone* being a "priest of the Most High God" was in Genesis 14:18 when Melchizedek came to Abram bringing him bread and wine.

Scripturally, Melchizedek seems to appear out of nowhere. We know from this passage he is king of the city of Salem (peace) and from Hebrews 7:2 that his name is translated "king of righteousness." We know nothing, however, of his relatives. While most scriptural characters are introduced as someone's son or daughter, this isn't true of Melchizedek. That's why, in Hebrews 7:3, he's described as being "without father, without mother, without genealogy, having neither beginning of days nor end of life, but made like the Son of God, remains a priest continually."

Jesus' appearance parallels his. His origins were a bit of a mystery to many people. His earthly origin was recognized easily enough. He came from the tribe of Judah and was a son of David through both Mary and Joseph (though Joseph didn't actually sire Him).

His heavenly origin, according to the author of Hebrews, is the order of Melchizedek. This was a claim many of Israel's leaders refused to accept. Levi would be superseded by Melchizedek because his priesthood had been confirmed long before Levi's—a priesthood which Psalm 110 declares would last forever.

When Christ arrives, He doesn't start a new order, He reinstates the one God already confirmed as His choice.

What does that mean for us? To be called a priest in the kingdom of God, to share in the priestly duties as Aaron's sons did with him, we no longer need to prove a heritage from Levi. If we are born of Christ, we are sons and daughters of the current and eternal Great High Priest, and our lineage comes from Him. If we are born of Christ, we are His sons and daughters and have become, as 1 Peter 2:9 says, "a chosen generation, a royal priesthood, a holy nation."

May we serve Him well for this special honor He gives us.

But He, because He continues forever,
has an unchangeable priesthood
(Hebrews 7:24).

Prayer: What an awesome God You are to make a way for me to serve with You as closely as the priests in the tabernacle did with Aaron. I came to You with neither heritage nor character to commend me, yet You connected Your genealogy with mine so there'd be a place for me in Your tent.

Deeper Still

Read Hebrews 7.
What does it mean to you to be part of the priesthood with Jesus? Journal your thoughts.

Week Three

Discussion Questions

We talked about the difference between eating and digesting and how that pertains to understanding God's words. We noticed the Holy Spirit's ability to illuminate the things of the Lord for us and appreciated the Lord's timeless nature. We considered how Jesus helps us pray at the altar of incense and discovered we need only trace our lineage to Jesus to share in His priesthood. Choose one or more of the following questions to consider on your own or discuss as a group.

1. What methods do you use to make sure you are fully digesting God's Word?
2. Describe a time the Holy Spirit illuminated something you otherwise wouldn't have been able to understand.
3. How does God's timeless nature affect your ability to pray and believe? How does knowing He's still in your past and already in your future affect your hope for the healing you need or the dreams you still have for your life?
4. Have you tried picturing Jesus pouring His incense over your prayers when you've brought your petitions to the Lord? How did that impact your faith?

5. Can you trace your priestly heritage to Jesus? If not, ask the group to pray with you to change that.
6. Questions? Insights? Look for "A Place for Me in God's Tent" on Facebook and join the conversation.

Week Four

Day 76

The Water of His Word

Before we begin, read Exodus 40:30–32 again

There's something annoyingly repetitive about ministry at the laver. Have you noticed it? The spot we remember scrubbing out yesterday seems to be the same blemish we're plunging under the faucet again today. It can be discouraging to discover just how frequently we need to return for a cleanup.

The apostle Paul understood the frustrations of dealing with seemingly never-ending cycles. In 2 Corinthians 12:7, he mentions a "thorn" in his flesh that simply won't go away. Whether it was a habit he struggled to conquer, a weakness in his health that refused to be healed, or a supernatural battle he faced again and again, God assures him He'd always supply enough grace to get through it.

I'm sure Paul would have preferred God simply zap the thorn and be done with it. I, too, would rather God help me deal decisively (and only once) with each character flaw the laver's mirror reveals. Instead, I find myself at the basin again and again, asking God to free me from this or that sin that so easily entangles me and give me the grace He promised Paul.

Here's where the form of the laver may give us a clue. The authors of *Commentary Critical and Explanatory on the*

Whole Bible describe the way Eastern people of the day normally washed their hands and feet. They held their extremities over a basin as they poured water over them. Because of this, Jamieson, Fausset, and Brown, suggest the laver in the tabernacle would likely have been a bronze bowl with a spout or spigot. Resting beneath, a shallow receptacle (a bronze trough) formed the basin. (Jamieson, Fausset and Brown 1997, 1:68)

Water that moves (as in a river or spring) is called "living water" in Scripture. Unlike still water in a cistern, it is fresh and life-giving. The bronze laver and base in operation present a picture of living water at work. Clean water pours from the spout. As it flows over skin, it captures dirt and carries it off to the basin below, leaving the hands and feet clean and refreshed.

Like water in a stream, God's word is always fresh. No matter how many times we read it, one more pass through the Scriptures can reveal something new, startling, surprising. These words are not just living, they're active, powerful, and capable of cutting right to the heart of a matter (Hebrews 4:12). We need them flowing over our thoughts again and again if they're going to soak into our hearts and dissolve our resistance.

God is not *frustrated* to see us back at the laver. He *expects* to see us there.

He doesn't expect us to conquer sin in a flash any more than He expected Israel to take the Promised Land all at once. God told them in Deuteronomy 7:22, victory would be "little by little," lest the "beasts of the field" overwhelm them. Any land we take in battle, in other words, we must also be capable of holding. Developing the skills to hold each bit of territory we conquer may require time and perseverance. We can trust God to know how much we can handle.

Philippians 4:8 recommends we set our minds on what is true, pure, lovely, and worthy of praise. That's good advice when ministering at the laver becomes tedious. As we scrub away at the same stubborn blemish, let's focus on what He's already made lovely in us, what aspects of our character He's already cleaned, already healed, already corrected. We can think on these things and remind ourselves of Philippians 1:6 — He promises to finish what He began in us.

My grace is sufficient for you, for
My strength is made perfect in weakness
(2 Corinthians 12:9).

Prayer: Dear Father, help me have patience with the good work You're doing in me. Help me remember You appointed these frequent visits to the laver of Your word so I won't be frustrated with the repetition.

Deeper Still

Read 2 Corinthians 12:7–10.
In your current struggle against sin, who do you think is more frustrated with your progress, you or God? What do you think He sees in your extended journey to wholeness that you aren't seeing? Journal your thoughts.

Day 77

The Nature of Linen

Before we begin, read Exodus 40:33

As the fence goes up around the courtyard, it surrounds us with yards and yards of gleaming white. In "Bridal Skirts" on Day 50, we connected linen's color to righteous good works. It's mode of manufacture, however, speaks of another type of righteousness — one which is inherent.

To understand this, let's step out of the courtyard a few minutes, to visit a field of flax. Flax is an airy herb about three feet high, topped with blue flowers during blooming season. To get the highest quality linen fibers from the flax, harvesters must rip it out by the roots before it's fully mature. They tie the stalks into bundles and plunge them under water, weighing them down with heavy rocks. This begins the "retting" process, where the plants soak for days. As they do, the layer of calcium and protein binding the inner fibers to the outer stalks gradually dissolves, enriching the local atmosphere with a fetid odor.

Eventually, they resurrect the bundles and spread the plants out to air dry several more days. Then it's time for "scutching." Grabbing the stalks, a handful at a time, workers hang them over a board and hammer them unmercifully with another piece of wood. Finally, they comb the shattered, broken stalks through a bed of nails to remove the last of the plant husks in a process called "heckling."

All that remains after this abuse are the innermost fibers of the flax—linen, as soft as hair. Far from destroying the linen, the retting and scutching and heckling serve to expose its fineness. This makes linen an apt symbol for the inner righteousness Jesus possessed.

His enemies badgered Him with evil intentions, tried to break Him with persecution and abuse, combed through His logic and tested His motives in an attempt to catch Him in some kind of error. In the end, they only proved Jesus was as pure, strong, and resilient as linen.

This kind of righteousness exemplifies an inner drive to stay true to God no matter what may happen—to give up everything in order to please Him. We know Jesus abstained from sinning, but we often don't appreciate what else He sacrificed to be God's perfect Lamb.

How many healing lines did He work through when He was already tired? How many meals did He give up so He could continue teaching and ministering when His Father told Him to keep going? How many detours in His ministry schedule did He accept because there was one more person God wanted to bless on the way to a major event? How many times did He rise while still exhausted because God asked Him to get up and minister?

We could never achieve a life of such pure devotion. Jesus not only died to make a place for us in God's tent, He offered His life to stand in for our own. Standing behind the fence of His white linen, we live "in Him". When God looks towards us, all He sees are the yards and yards of Christ's righteousness surrounding us, and He is satisfied.

For you died, and your life is hidden with Christ in God
(Colossians 3:3).

Prayer: Lord Jesus, my gratitude seems insufficient to give You proper honor. Thank You for making a place for me in God's tent and letting me hide behind Your righteousness.

Deeper Still

Read 1 Corinthians 1:26–31.

Paul notes few of us come to God with anything to recommend ourselves. Jesus, however "became for us" all the things we needed—wisdom, righteousness, and all the rest. What does being "in Christ" like this mean to you? Journal your thoughts.

Day 78

The Offerings Begin

Before we begin, read Exodus 40:29, and Leviticus 1:1–2

The tent is in place, its parts are assembled and furniture aligned. It's finally time for ministry to begin.

So far, we've seen Christ represented in the tabernacle, its furniture, and in the high priest himself. Today, we begin considering what the offerings have to say about Him. Before we go into detail, let's look at the offerings in general.

All the sacrifices will share a common purpose—to act as substitutes or stand-ins in some capacity for the worshipper. While they'll differ in particulars, Alfred Edersheim classifies each offering in one of two categories. They will either be given *in* communion with God or *for* communion with Him. (Edersheim 1994, 77) The burnt, grain, and peace offerings celebrate fellowship with God that is intact, while the sin and trespass offerings serve to restore fellowship that has been broken.

To present their offerings, worshippers approach from the east, through the gate of the courtyard. As they stand before the brazen altar, they face west, toward the holy place. The door to the tabernacle is before them and beyond the door stands the ark of God's presence. Worshippers, in essence, come face-to-face with God when they bring their gifts.

They lay hands on the sacrifice and, in that moment of personal contact, gift and giver identify with one another and share in each other's attributes. The good and acceptable qualities of the offering suddenly belong to the person who presents it, while the unacceptable qualities of the worshipper are accounted to the sacrifice.

A portion of each offering is separated to God. Only His share burns on the bronze altar, producing a smoke carrying "a sweet savor" to Him. Any part of the sacrifice bearing what is abhorrent to God burns outside the camp on a different fire. Whatever isn't destined for one of these fires will be shared with priests and people.

Each type of offering illustrates something different about Messiah's role as the Lamb of God. The depth and breadth of His sacrifice cannot be illustrated in a single sacrifice. So, God instituted multiple varieties of offerings, to be handled in different ways, in order to demonstrate what Messiah's life, death, and resurrection would mean for us.

The people of Moses' day had no Scriptures to study, but they could "read" about God in the ritual playing out in front of them. As they leaned heavily on the sacrifice, watched it die and burn, they not only gained an understanding of the seriousness of sin but an appreciation for the substitution taking place. They saw the sacrifice being judged in their place with their own eyes.

Time and culture separate us from this multi-sensory experience today. As a result, we often minimize not only the reality of sin, but the justice it deserves and the danger it poses to us. Without a thorough understanding of the sacrificial system, our appreciation for what Jesus has done for us lacks dimension and emotional impact. So, let's take a hard look at the offerings and discover why the author of Hebrews called ours "so great a salvation."

> *Christ came as High Priest of the good things to come,*
> *with the greater and more perfect tabernacle not made*
> *with hands. . . . Not with the blood of goats and calves,*
> *but with His own blood He entered the Most Holy Place*
> *(Hebrews 9:11–12).*

Prayer: Heavenly Father, You have not required me to actually see the grizzly scene of Christ's sacrifice. Help me to grasp how serious this transaction is between the Lamb of God and me.

Deeper Still

Read Hebrews 9:23–10:10.

The author quotes an Old Testament passage saying God didn't desire sacrifices of goats and bulls. There was, however, a "body" He would accept—His son's. What differences do you see between Jesus and the animal sacrifices at this point? Journal your thoughts.

Day 79

Acceptance Assured

Before we begin, read Leviticus 1:3–9

Many different sacrifices are described throughout Scripture, but they're pretty much all based off the five forms listed in Leviticus — the burnt, sin, peace, bread, and trespass offerings.

We'll begin our discoveries with the burnt offering. The Israelites were already familiar with this type of sacrifice. Aside from their first Passover lamb, it was the only kind of offering they had thus far presented to God.

As we step up to the altar with our bull, a knife flashes forth and the animal drops to its knees and dies as its life pours out. The priests capture its blood in bowls and splash it around the altar. Then, as if to verify the offering we brought was truly perfect, they begin slashing the beast apart and tossing all its pieces on the altar. The burnt offering's head, legs, internal organs — indeed, it's whole being — lays exposed and open to examination.

None of the sacrifice is reserved for human consumption. It all belongs to God. The burnt offering's entire being has been wholly given over to God. The fire licking at its flesh validates God's approval of the sacrifice and His satisfaction in every part.

What is this gruesome scene all about? In Leviticus 1:3, "He shall bring it to the entrance of the tent of meeting, that he may be accepted before the LORD" (ESV).

Acceptance. Who doesn't want that?

Psalm 24:3–4 asks, "Who may ascend into the hill of the LORD? Or who may stand in His holy place? He who has clean hands and a pure heart." To stand in God's holy place, we need to be clean and pure. But who can claim to have unsullied hands or an absolutely flawless heart? None of us. We need a substitute, or we'll never qualify to draw near to God.

Enter the burnt offering. This sacrifice satisfies the requirements for outward perfection because the priests have visually examined it. As they remove its organs and lay them on the fire, they prove its inner perfection as well. If God accepts the burnt offering, the worshipper is likewise accepted.

In Mark 12:30, Jesus says the first great commandment is to love God with all our heart, soul, and strength. The burnt offering seems to express this kind of total devotion—its scattered pieces crying out, "Search me, O God . . . and see if there is any wicked way in me" (Psalm 139:23–24).

Bulls and calves, however, can be no more than placeholders for a person. Only a human sacrifice can fully satisfy God's requirements for human beings. The true burnt offering, the one God would accept at His heavenly altar, is one who not only obeys God's law as to its letter, but as to its spirit.

Jesus proved His righteousness is both inner and outer—one of being, not just doing. His inner nature is always tuned in to the Father. His mind and heart and strength, like those pieces of the burnt offering scattered across the surface of the altar, have been tested and proved pure.

If we were tested against the first commandment, we'd never pass on our own, so we still need a burnt offering today. One moment of deviation, one episode of choosing to satisfy our personal desire before satisfying the Lord and we'd be rejected—stamped "unacceptable." We need a stand-in who can live the wholly dedicated life we can't. As we trust in Jesus and lean on Him, it is as though we've laid hands on the sacrifice. We identify with Him as our burnt offering and His acceptance becomes our own.

We will never match Jesus in devotion, no matter how we try, but that's okay. Matthew 10:24–25 says it's enough to try and be like Him. He lived a devoted life *for* us so that, as we stumble along in our imitation of Him, we can be confident our failures won't disqualify us from His tabernacle. In Christ, we are always accepted by the Father.

He made us accepted in the Beloved
(Ephesians 1:6).

Prayer: When I think of how difficult it is for me to resist satisfying my own desires, I am undone by the strength of Your resolve, Lord Jesus. Teach me how to increase my own devotion to God.

Deeper Still

Read Ephesians 1:3–6.
Notice Paul says God chose us to be "holy and without blame" in Christ. Picture Jesus stepping onto the altar in your place, receiving God's stamp of approval and handing it over to you. How does that encourage you to strive harder to be like Him? Journal your thoughts.

Day 80

Establishing the Substitute

Before we begin, read Leviticus 1:10–13

The courtyard is bustling with activity and noise. People shout and bulls bellow. Lambs and goat kids bleat their protest as turtle doves coo and flutter in their cages. While they bring burnt offerings of varying sorts, the people present them in similar ways.

If we were one of them, we'd begin by contributing our sacrifice of our own free will. If we bring a burnt offering out of some sense of duty or coercion, we might demonstrate our fear of God, but not our love for Him.

We'd also bring an offering from our own substance. (Edersheim 1994, 78) King David understood this. When he wanted to build a temple for God in Jerusalem, someone else owned the land he wanted to use for it. Though the landowner offered to give it to the king in 2 Samuel 24:24, David refused to take it for free. "I will surely buy it from you for a price; nor will I offer burnt offerings to the LORD my God with that which costs me nothing."

When we bring our burnt offering, we present it "at the door" of the tabernacle. The wording is, perhaps, a bit confusing, because the people of Moses' day only approach as far as the altar with their gift. No one but the priests actually go beyond it and laver to stand right next to the door. From our position before the brazen altar, however, we can see the door to the tabernacle and we're very aware that the one standing behind it is the Holy One of Israel.

Before the sacrifice is slain, we firmly lay hands upon it — publicly and personally identifying with it and claiming it as our own. Without this step, no substitution will take place. The holiness of the offering will have no opportunity to transfer to us. The sacrifice itself might be accepted as spotless, but we gain nothing by presenting it.

As we noted before, animals are merely placeholders for the Messiah they foreshadow. Jesus eventually reveals Himself as the Lamb of God — the ultimate of all burnt offerings. As we present ourselves at God's door of our own free will, lean on Jesus (trusting and believing Him), and claim Him as our own, He becomes the burnt offering and our substitute at the heavenly altar. Because He is accepted, so are we.

How about you? Have you come to God's door, presenting Jesus as the sacrifice for your life? Have you touched Him in your heart and declared Him openly as your substitute and burnt offering? Then rejoice and receive His stamp of approval as your own.

I say to you, whoever confesses Me before men, him the Son of Man also will confess before the angels of God (Luke 12:8).

Prayer: Lord Jesus, I do not like the feel of this — that I should profit from what cost You so dearly. Nevertheless, Lord, to whom else can I go? I accept the gift of You. I accept You as my substitute. Thank You for sharing Your acceptance with me.

Deeper Still

Read Romans 10:9–13.

When the people brought their sacrifices to the altar, they were making a public statement about what they believed. When Paul speaks about "confessing" Jesus in these verses, he's implying a similarly public relationship with Him. In what kind of circumstances do you find it difficult to live your faith out loud? Why do you think that is? Journal your thoughts.

Week Four

Discussion Questions

We talked about the repetitiveness of the ministry of the laver and how Jesus' life was perfectly reflected in the production of fine linen. We began looking at how Christ is represented in the sacrifices at the bronze altar and considered how the acceptability of the sacrifice is conferred to the one presenting the offering to the Lord. Choose one or more of the following questions to consider on your own or discuss as a group.

1. Do you allow others to help with those stubborn blots in your character or do you insist on scouring away at them by yourself? How might you begin opening up to safe friends to gain more support?
2. Jesus went through "retting," "scutching," and "heckling" to produce the "fine linen" of His righteousness. How have your trials been similar and what kinds of final products did they produce? How did these difficult steps in the process affect your fruitfulness?
3. Why was it necessary for a person to lay hands on their sacrifice at the altar? How do we "identify" with Jesus when we lean on Him as our sacrificial Lamb today?
4. Have you been public about your relationship with the Lord or have you tried to hide your visits to the

altar from the crowd in the courtyard? What advice can you give one another about being more open about your faith?

5. Questions? Insights? Look for "A Place for Me in God's Tent" on Facebook and join the conversation.

Week Five

Day 81

Becoming Living Sacrifices

Before we begin, read Leviticus 1:14–17

We notice some particular characteristics of all these animal types coming before the altar. The bull ripples with strength, the lamb carries the aura of gentle submissiveness, and the dove flutters a whisper-like message of peace and innocence.

As the promised Messiah, Christ is known as having all these attributes. He dedicated all His strength and labors to God, submitted His will entirely to the Father, and maintained His innocence His whole life. In John 8:28–29 He tells His disciples, "I do nothing of Myself; but as My Father taught Me, I speak these things. . . . I always do those things that please Him."

A fully devoted life is what produces the sweet savor of the burnt offering's smoke in the tabernacle. Had Jesus taken one step for Himself, had He satisfied one personal desire, He would have disqualified Himself as a fit substitute for human beings on the heavenly altar. He lived a sacrificial life, daily subjecting the whole of Himself to His Father.

Though we don't qualify as substitutes for other people the way Jesus did, we are still called to imitate Him. "I beseech you therefore, brethren, by the mercies of God, that you present your bodies a living sacrifice, holy, acceptable to God, which is your reasonable service" (Romans 12:1).

Following His example is no mean feat. As Andrew Jukes points out in *The Law of the Offerings*, "Man's duty to God is not the giving up of one faculty, but the entire surrender of all." (Jukes 1966, 63) Our bodies, souls, and spirits are to be as totally submitted to God as the head, body, and innards of the burnt offering are to the fire on the brazen altar.

Now, I *want* to be completely dedicated to God. I even succeed for limited periods of time. But to *never* give in to myself? That's something I cannot imagine. What hope, then, do I have in presenting myself as an acceptable living sacrifice to God?

Here's where that moment of contact at the altar becomes so important. As we lean on Jesus by fully trusting in Him, we become like the worshippers laying hands on the bull or lamb in the tabernacle. Our hearts acknowledge Him as our burnt offering and His perfect dedication is counted as our own. Our inability to stay true will no longer threaten our welcome in God's dwelling place.

This sets us free to imitate Him out of love rather than fear, giving our strength, our wills, and our innocence upon His altar as our own burnt offerings. Our inevitable mistakes along the way may frustrate us and send us to the laver again and again, but they don't need to disturb our sense of peace with God. As we advance and retreat in the struggle toward more complete dedication, we can trust Him to secure our place in His tent.

I beseech you therefore, brethren, by the mercies of God, that you present your bodies a living sacrifice, holy, acceptable to God, which is your reasonable service
(Romans 12:1).

Prayer: Lord Jesus, help me give ever more and more of myself to You as I learn from Your example.

Deeper Still

Read Romans 12:9–21

Everything Paul talks about in this passage requires the offering of our labors, will, and/or innocence to God as we serve our brethren. Each part of his admonition requires we give something of ourselves for the sake of another. Which of these areas is most difficult for you? How can you better imitate Christ as a living sacrifice? Journal your thoughts.

Day 82

A Gift Shared

Before we begin, read Leviticus 2:1–10

The burnt offering we talked about yesterday was called *olah* — that which goes up. The entire sacrifice (aside from its hide) went up in smoke as God's portion.

Today's grain offering, on the other hand, is a bit different. God asks only its first handful be devoted to Him. While His portion goes into the fire, the rest is presented to the priests as their food. No wonder the Hebrew word for grain offering is *minchah* — gift.

The "gift" of grain is a way for God to demonstrate His concern for the needs of His people. Had we been among that crowd in the tabernacle, we might have felt a startling change in focus. Except for our experience with the Passover lamb, we'd have been unfamiliar with offerings that went to the altar and then came back to us. Might it hint at a Messiah who would both go to God and return to His people?

Jesus says as much when He speaks to His disciples in John 16:16 and says, "A little while, and you will not see Me; and again a little while, and you will see Me, because I go to the Father."

The various forms of the grain offering — raw grain straight from the stalk, flour ground fine, or cakes baked or fried — foreshadow the Messiah as well. As grain, He would be the first fruits of the harvest to come. As flour, He would be sifted by persecution. As baked wafers or cakes, He would suffer the fires of affliction. And, because so much of the offering was returned to the priests, the bulk of Messiah's service to the Father would involve nourishing His people.

1 Kings 17:8–16 recounts the story of a widow living in the community of Zarephath during a famine. She had nothing in her house but a bit of flour and oil when the prophet Elijah stopped by. If she would feed him with this little handful first, he told her, her supply of oil and flour wouldn't run out until rain returned to the land. By giving the prophet her bread, it was like presenting a grain offering to the God who sent Elijah. Then, as though given back from the altar, the larger portion went to the widow, enabling her to survive the famine.

Jesus gave similar demonstrations of the Father seeing to the needs of His people in the New Testament. In Matthew 14:14–21, five thousand of Christ's followers were hungry. They brought a handful of food (five loaves and two fish) to Jesus who presented it to the Father. As though receiving the bread offering back, the people consumed the larger portion in return.

Oh, why do we worry God will be stingy with us? There will be times our sacrifice will be as a burnt offering, going wholly to the Lord, but countless are the days He'll follow our handful-sized gift with abundance poured into our laps.

> For the bread of God is He who comes down
> from heaven and gives life to the world
> (John 6:33).

Prayer: How generous you are, Father, and how often I forget that. Open my heart to give without fear to a God who never forgets my needs and is so thoroughly trustworthy.

Deeper Still

Read Matthew 14:14–21.

When was the last time God gave you more than you gave Him? How does that match up with the story of the bread offering? Is there someone you can encourage today who needs to know God cares about their needs? Journal your thoughts.

Day 83

Bread and Wine

*Before we begin, read Leviticus 2:11–16
and Exodus 29:38–42*

There's an element noticeably missing from the grain offering that is present in all the other offerings—blood. You may have noticed from previous readings that the priests splashed the blood of the burnt offering around the altar. For other sacrifices, they'll paint it on the altar's horns, pour it at its base, sprinkle it before the veil, drip it on the horns of the altar of incense, and even sprinkle on the ark itself on the Great Day of Atonement.

No matter how we grind or sift or bake or fry the grain offering, however, we get no blood out of it. We read in Leviticus 17:11 that God calls blood the "life of the flesh," and that lifeblood is the only thing that qualifies to make "atonement for the soul." It was a holy substance which God had been telling them since Genesis 9:4 they weren't to consume, whether the blood came from a sacrifice or from an animal used as food.

As it turns out the bread offering has a partner at the altar. As we read in Exodus 29:38–42, a drink offering accompanies it. In fact, almost every time the bread offering is mentioned in Scripture, its drink is noted as well.

The drink offering is wine, not surprisingly a scriptural symbol for blood. In Luke 22:19–20, for example, as Jesus shares His last supper with His disciples, He equates the wine to His blood.

Raising bread and cup together, He seems to dramatize the very grain offering He would soon become — His life given as the first fruits or handful of grain, and His blood ready to be poured out in death. Like the high priest sharing the rest of the bread with his brethren, Jesus turned to His disciples, and gave bread and wine to them.

The partnership of grain and wine offerings appears today in the ritual of communion or Eucharist. We recognize His flesh in the bread and let Him become food for us by means of His words and His life. We recognize His blood in our communion drink — acknowledging His life given in exchange for our own.

The next time you share in a communion meal, let your imagination travel to the tabernacle. Picture Christ as the unleavened bread at the altar, His life as the drink offering poured out at the base. As you eat the bread, think of His labors on your behalf — each action chosen to clarify your understanding of God's love for you, each word chosen to nourish your soul. With the cup, see His life not just poured out *for* you but poured *into* you — strength for the journey, His life pledged for yours.

Don't let the somber note of His death leave a sad aftertaste as you finish the drink offering. Wine is not just a symbol for blood and life, verses such as Psalm 104:15 use it as a symbol for joy. Christ did indeed die for us, but He also picked His life back up when His work was done. It was for the joy that lay before Him He ran this race of becoming our substitute at God's heavenly altar. That joy was sharing His meal with us.

For as often as you eat this bread and drink this cup, you
proclaim the Lord's death till He comes
(1 Corinthians 11:26).

Prayer: Lord Jesus, thank You for the gift of Yourself. I treasure the way Your words and deeds feed my soul. I soak up the life You pour into my spirit.

Deeper Still

Read 1 Corinthians 11:23–26.

Let's think of the bread as Jesus' life in the flesh and the wine as His life poured out unto death. Why is it important to show these two together? How does the way He lived His life benefit us and what different benefit do we receive from His death? Journal your thoughts.

Day 84

Fellowship Intact

Before we begin, read Leviticus 3:1–11

Though these early chapters of Leviticus describe the different sacrifices, they don't present them in the order they will go into the fire during the daily offerings. Once tabernacle ministry begins, however, the capstone of the ceremony will be the peace offering, when the priests pile it on top of the other sacrifices in celebration of having their fellowship with God restored. Alfred Edersheim called it, appropriately, "the offering of completion." (Edersheim 1994, 99)

As we noticed before, only God's portion of each sacrifice burns on the brazen altar. For the burnt offering, He claimed the entire animal. For the grain offering, He required the first handful. With the peace offering, He asks for the fat and kidneys to go up in smoke.

Why these particular pieces?

David Levy suggests fat is a sign of an animal's health and vigor and therefore the richest part of its body. (Levy 2003, 115) How many of us regard the fat encircling our middle a sign of abundance and overflow we'd rather not display quite so openly? God claims as His own these pieces which so vividly convey a sense of richness and liberality.

At first, the fat might not seem like a large portion of the sacrifice, but this was no paltry piece of lard going into the fire. The fat from a sheep's tail alone could have weighed as much as eight to ten pounds. (Levy 2003, 115) Can you imagine the flare-ups on the bronze altar when these grease-laden slabs hit the griddle?

What about the kidneys, then? These hide deep in the body cavity and will be among the last of the organs to come out when the sacrifice is cut apart — signifying something more like the innermost being of the animal. (Thomas 1998) In fact, the word used for "kidneys" in the peace offering reappears in Psalm 139:13 as "inward parts," when the psalmist speaks of being formed in his mother's womb.

Isn't this so like the Lamb of God? Coming into the world as our ultimate peace offering, Jesus gives the choicest part of Himself to the Father on our behalf. All God's requirements for human inner purity are met in Him. He is wholly approved in body, soul, and spirit. When we accept Jesus as our substitute and peace offering, God judges His inward parts rather than ours and He is satisfied. Because the sacrificial Lamb is approved, so are we.

The presentation of the peace offering is a celebration of all that the other sacrifices accomplish. The sin and trespass offerings (which we'll look at later) carry away what is abhorrent to God. The burnt offering provides us with acceptance. The grain and wine offerings bring nourishment and strength. But sealing it all, the peace offering declares the work complete and celebrates the restoration of our fellowship with God.

Our reunification with the Father is complete in Christ. Every part of our relationship which was broken is healed in Him — down to the innermost parts of our hearts.

With God fully satisfied in every way, with our communion with Father, Son and Holy Spirit fully restored, what shall be impossible for us now?

Therefore, having been justified by faith, we have peace with God through our Lord Jesus Christ (Romans 5:1).

Prayer: Lord God, I am in awe. You have done everything, *everything* to make my place with You in this tent secure. How can I thank You enough for this inexpressible gift?

Deeper Still

Read Colossians 1:19–23.

God has found a way, in spite of the "wicked works" that kept us separated from Him, to reconcile us with God. Look through the various definitions for the word "reconcile" in a dictionary. Which of them best fits what God has done for you? Journal your thoughts.

Day 85

The Law and the Sin Offering

Before we begin, read Leviticus 4:1–10

God described the burnt, bread, and peace offerings to us before the sin offering, even though their order of presentation at the altar will be a bit different. It's as though He's extended His olive branch to us before He deals with the hard stuff — reassuring us His ultimate aim is to have us dwelling closely with Him in His tent.

While a burnt offering was all Israel needed before they departed from Egypt, something has changed to make more extensive sacrifices necessary. Moses didn't just bring the tabernacle designs down the mountain with him in Exodus 25–31, he brought the Law.

Nothing demonstrates how crooked something is like placing it next to a ruler. As we stand ourselves up against the Ten Commandments, we can see just how far off we are from being straight and upright. While the Law clarifies what God wants from us, it also defines what is wrong and gives it a name. Sin.

Our muddy feet and soiled hearts are going to make life inside His tabernacle impossible for us. Like Adam and Eve in the garden of Eden, we can now see how naked we are. With God's law etched clearly in stone before us, guilt and shame will continually shake accusing fingers at us — chasing us from His presence like brooms frightening mice.

The apostle Paul would explain it this way in Romans 5:13: "Until the law sin was in the world, but sin is not imputed when there is no law." In other words, even though God's people had done things contrary to His desires before the tabernacle arrived, they weren't charged with breaking His Law until He wrote it out before them.

So, up to the brazen altar comes the sin offering. We lay hands on this sacrifice as we've done with the others. Once more, the blade drives deep, the priest collects the blood, and splashes it around the altar. He slashes the body open and wrenches out the fat, liver, and kidneys to cast into the fire on the bronze altar as God's portion.

As we noticed last time, the fat, kidneys, and now the fatty portion of the liver are the richest, most valuable pieces of the sacrifice. The fire of their burning presents a picture of a sinless inward life presented to God, declared "not guilty" by Him, and accepted.

We can never obey God's Law perfectly through our own efforts. According to Jeremiah 17:9, human hearts are "desperately wicked." Our inner being is the battlefield for what Andrew Jukes calls the "ever-remaining, ever-struggling sin within us." (Jukes 1966, 152) We may strive to bring our hearts into subjection, as Paul writes in 1 Corinthians 9:27, but we'll never quite get there in our own strength.

Bulls and lambs and goats would only serve as sin offerings until the real Lamb of God arrived. Jesus Christ, the Son of God and Son of man would stand in for us before God's judgment seat. Stretch out your hands and lean on the sacrifice. Claim Him as your sin offering and let Him share His "not guilty" verdict with you.

For what the law was powerless to do in that it was weakened by the sinful nature, God did by sending his own Son in the likeness of sinful man to be a sin offering (Romans 8:3 NIV).

Prayer: Thank You for being my sin offering, Jesus. Thank You for keeping my place secure as I struggle day by day to bring every part of my heart into agreement with Your will.

Deeper Still

Read Romans 7:15–8:4.

Our inner self is a battleground. What we "ought" to do is always fighting against what we "want" to do. As you struggle to become more like Jesus, remember He's holding your place in the tabernacle. How does that encourage you to pick yourself up after a failure and try again? Journal your thoughts.

Week Five

Discussion Questions

This week we looked at the fully devoted life of the burnt offering and the remembrance of the needs of God's people in the grain offering. We noticed life poured out in the drink offering while remembering its connection to joy. We touched on the joy of the peace offering and the somber meaning behind the sin offering. Choose one or more of the following questions to consider on your own or discuss as a group.

1. Andrew Jukes suggested the bull, lamb and turtle dove of the burnt offering represented strength, submissiveness, and innocence being offered to the Lord. Which of these aspects of your life is most difficult to dedicate to Him? Discuss how you might help one another with your weaknesses.
2. If we're going to imitate Christ in the grain offering, then we'll be as much in need of the oil poured over us as He was. Pray together that the Holy Spirit would drizzle over you as olive oil over the grain offering.
3. If you're comfortable doing so, share a communion meal with each other and talk about what it means to you having Christ share His life with you.
4. The peace offering was a celebration of fellowship restored. What is your greatest joy in knowing you've

been reconciled with God? How do you celebrate that joy?

5. Do you have particular desires that constantly tempt you to do what you know is wrong? Even though you resist them, do struggle with guilt? Pray for one another to lay even this inner sense of guilt on Christ so He can carry it away on the back of our great sin offering.

6. Questions? Insights? Look for "A Place for Me in God's Tent" on Facebook and join the conversation.

Week Six

Day 86

The *Saraph* Fire

Before we begin, read Leviticus 4:11-21

As the priest prepares the sin offering, we notice he divides it into two groups. One set of body parts burns inside the tabernacle and the other is sent outside.

Two different Hebrew words describe how the two sets are consumed. God's portion — its inward parts — *qatar* on the brazen altar in a fire producing a sweet-smelling savor to the LORD. The rest of the sacrifice — its head, legs, hide, and entrails — *saraph* outside the camp, in a fierce, all-consuming blaze suggestive of God's wrath poured out.

The sin offering isn't established to address specific acts of disobedience (those will be dealt with by the trespass offering). Instead, it's God's answer to the very nature of sin itself — that "ever-remaining, ever-struggling sin within us" we mentioned before. (Jukes 1966, 152)

Evil intentions are buried seeds lying within our hearts. A splash of opportunity, a dash of fertilizing temptation, and they sprout overnight into actions we regret. Once that evil desire has been conceived in our hearts, James 1:15 says, "it gives birth to sin; and sin, when it is full-grown, brings forth death."

We fight an inner battle between our human nature's desire for self-satisfaction and the yearning of Christ's nature within us for total devotion to God. The battle is great because the stakes couldn't be higher, as the fate of the outer portion of the sin offering demonstrates.

Deuteronomy 30:19 tells us the choice between life and death is our own. We choose life inside God's tent by accepting the sin offering He's already approved. We choose death when we reject His great gift. In Matthew 13:41–42, Christ warns that, at some point, He will weed out of the kingdom all who cause sin or do evil and send them to a *saraph*-like fire that makes teeth gnash and voices wail. If we allow sin to remain on our heavenly accounts, we'll go with it to sin's final resting place.

That needn't happen when such a great opportunity is before us. As we noted earlier, the sin offering is called *chattaah* in Hebrew—"the sinful thing." When, in 2 Corinthians 5:21, the apostle Paul says God "made Him who knew no sin to be sin for us," he is talking about Christ becoming our *chattaah*.

When Jesus was taken outside the city of Jerusalem to die, He went the way of the outer portion of the sin offering, outside the camp. On the cross, He experienced the desperation and terror of total separation from the Father, as though suffering in the *saraph* fire. His cry from the cross in Matthew 27:46—"My God, My God, why have You forsaken Me?"—demonstrates the depth of His distress at being apart from His Father.

Though we experience seasons when God feels far away, they don't compare to knowing the pain of total separation from God Jesus suffered in our place.

All praise to the Lamb of God who gave Himself as *chattaah* for us. He carries our sin away, yet represents us at the altar, sending a sweet savor to the Almighty on our behalf. He simultaneously shares with us His reputation and takes away our shame. How could we be saved any more completely?

And so Jesus also suffered outside the city gate to
make the people holy through his own blood
(Hebrews 13:12 NIV).

Prayer: Lord Jesus, thank You for suffering the horror of separation from God in my place. It's hard to believe You would do such a thing for me. May my life always reflect my appreciation for such a glorious gift.

Deeper Still

Read Psalm 22.

As you read this Psalm, picture Jesus declaring it with His final breaths from the cross. Though He clearly felt the pain of separation from the Father, notice how confident He was God would draw Him out of it in the end. How can you follow His example the next time God feels far away from you? Journal your thoughts.

Day 87

Forgive Us Our Trespasses

Before we begin, read Leviticus 5:14–19

We've dealt with the overall sinful nature of our hearts, but now we need to do something about our individual acts of sin. These meet their match in the trespass offering.

Much of the book of Leviticus clarifies what kinds of sinful acts might be counted as trespasses, but the big difference between this offering and any of the others is its requirement for restitution. The trespass offering will not only bring satisfaction to God for ways we've offended Him, but to human victims of our wrong behaviors as well.

We may think our sin affects no one but ourselves, but the instructions for this offering indicate otherwise. Trespasses produce suffering, loss, or damage, either for God or for man. Therefore, this offering needs to do more than provide forgiveness for the perpetrator.

Leviticus 5:15 and :17 address offenses against God first. He becomes the injured party when we commit wrongdoing "in regard to the holy things of the LORD" or "forbidden to be done by the commandments of the LORD." When we misuse what is holy to God or flout His laws, we hurt Him first.

Our transgressions cause Him to suffer loss. Have you ever looked back on a season in your life and mourned how much time you wasted going the wrong way? Regretted the opportunities you missed by mishandling or ignoring things pertaining to God? Did you grieve the cost accrued to your family or friends because you were so busy satisfying yourself you had no time for them or for God? Those trespasses deprived God of opportunities, delayed His plans, and hurt His heart until you came back to your senses and returned to Him.

The ram of the trespass offering works forgiveness for the human transgressor, but restitution for the injured party takes different forms. To recompense God, tabernacle shekels make a reappearance. Silver coins, of course, can't actually make up for God's losses at our hands. He already owns the cattle on a thousand hills. Why would He ask for money?

Earlier we noticed the connection between the shekels and redeemed lives in the tabernacle. In "Melted and Molded" on Day 38, we discovered the importance of bringing coins measuring up to the quality of silver in the tabernacle shekels. Together, these details speak of a life free of impurities given to God. Though the silver shekels represent our lives in the tabernacle, they only do so because of an exchange.

Our lives could never come out of the furnace of life pure enough to present ourselves as tabernacle-quality silver. So, what can we offer God as a restitution for the loss our trespasses cause Him?

We offer the blemish-free life already given up for us — the silver shekel of Messiah. Once more Jesus steps up to be our substitute, giving back to God what we could never restore on our own — the wasted years, the opportunities lost, the grief we've caused Him.

Halleluiah to a Messiah big enough, valuable enough, and good enough to fill the potholes our sins leave behind.

You were not redeemed with corruptible things,
like silver or gold, from your aimless conduct . . . but
with the precious blood of Christ, as of a lamb without
blemish and without spot
(1 Peter 1:18–19).

Prayer: Heavenly Father, when I think what I've cost You in resisting, hesitating, and disobeying, I am undone. Please accept the only trespass offering worthy of paying my debt to You—Your own ram, Your own silver, Jesus Christ.

Deeper Still

Read Psalm 32:1–5.

Can you rejoice with David in this Psalm? He only felt relief when he opened up to the Lord and confessed his trespasses. Have you had times you've held onto sin too long? What convinced you to bring it to the altar? Journal your thoughts.

Day 88

As We Forgive Others

Before we begin, read Leviticus 6:1–7.

While tabernacle shekels count as retribution for the Lord, something else is required for trespasses committed against human beings. Stolen items must be returned, extortion must be repaid, lies must be corrected, what was lost must be restored along with an extra fifth added to its full value. Only after restitution is made with his neighbor can the guilty party bring his trespass offering to the Lord and receive forgiveness.

There's a familiar New Testament ring to these instructions. "If you bring your gift to the altar, and there remember that your brother has something against you, leave your gift there before the altar, and go your way. First be reconciled to your brother, and then come and offer your gift" (Matthew 5:23–24).

God expects us to be accountable not only to Him for our actions, but to our neighbor. If we've harmed someone, it's our responsibility to face up to it and make restitution, if there is an appropriate way to do so. Jesus is willing to be our restitution to God when we trespassed against Him, so we should be willing to offer reparations to those we wrong.

Sometimes, we are the victim, however. What if the one who hurt us either makes no attempt to pay back

TERRY MURPHY

their debt, or offers a restitution inadequate to our loss? What then?

What if we ask Jesus to do for our offender what He's already done for us and be the stand-in for the trespass offering for the one who hurt us?

This may seem an odd notion, but some trespasses inflict such pain and cost us so greatly that no human being could present sufficient compensation to make up for the deficit they caused. We can get so fixated on requiring restitution from the one who actually racked up the debt that we miss opportunities to make a better deal with a substitute.

Jesus has the ability to make the kind of restitution we need. If we let Him take over the debt of our offender, He can bring real healing to our lives.

Of course, letting Christ take over the restitution part of the trespass offering means allowing Him to manage their forgiveness as well. Giving up our claim against our transgressor means trusting God to do what's right concerning justice.

We cannot hold two different people responsible for the same debt. So who will we choose to cover it? The person who actually owes us — but may or may not have the ability to make adequate restitution — or the Son of God, who is able to give exceedingly abundantly more than we could ask or imagine?

If we let our offender go free, Jesus will not only make up for our loss, He will add an unbelievable fifth to it as well. Let us claim Jesus as our substitute for the whole trespass offering and save ourselves from getting stuck in unforgiveness.

Only He, after all, can make right what has gone horribly wrong.

Bless those who curse you, and pray for those who spitefully use you
(Luke 6:28).

Prayer: Father God, help me choose wisely in deciding whom to hold accountable for trespasses committed against me. Set me free to release others from their debt and trust Jesus with making restitution.

Deeper Still

Read Luke 6:27–36.

How does considering Jesus as your restitution-maker help with the idea of turning the other cheek and forgiving others? Journal your thoughts.

Day 89

The Sacrifice on Display

Before we begin, read Leviticus 9:1–22.

Now that we've learned a bit about the types of sacrifices, let's push our way through the crowds and watch them being offered.

As we take our position before the bronze altar, the sin offering comes forward. Several priests reach out their hands to touch its head. Sunlight flashes off the blade of a knife and the beast goes down. A priest pours its blood at the base of the altar and paints it on the brazen horns, then throws its inward parts onto the coals. Other priests hoist the carcass and cart it out of the camp.

A bull bellows and we turn to see the burnt offering pulled to the altar. A crowd of priests coalesces around it and the knife swings again. Cutting it apart, a priest hurls it piece by piece into the fire.

Handfuls of grain offering rain down on the meat and pop in the flames. Wine sloshes out of its cups, drawing rivers of red around the altar's base.

The peace offering steps forward to be slain and separated. Its fat and kidneys land heavily on top of the burning pile. The burnt offering is now sandwiched between the fatty portions of sin and peace offerings. Fire leaps in the midst of the rendering fat, its snapping flames sounding like God's applause. As the smoke rises, the sacrifices disappear in its cloud.

This is the sight of our fellowship with God being restored. We can now join the congregation's celebration and feast together on bread and meat reserved for us from the altar. No longer does anything stand between us and the deep places of the tent. It is finished.

As dramatic as this scene has been, it's nothing but a shadow of what happens when Jesus presents Himself as the Lamb of God. As is proper for any offering, He first submits Himself for inspection—initially to the Jewish leaders, but then to the Gentiles. In Matthew 26:59–65, the Sanhedrin finds nothing against Him except the false charge of blasphemy. In Luke 23:4–22 Pilate pronounces Him innocent three times.

Before He is slain, hands must be laid upon the sacrifice to allow for a transfer to take place. In Mark 14:65, Jewish hands pummel Him in the presence of the high priest. In Mark 15:17–19, Gentile hands beat Him under the auspices of the governor. Having been touched by both Jew and Gentile, Jesus is ready to offer Himself for all mankind at the heavenly altar.

Together Jew and Gentile flay open His body. Together, they usher Jesus outside the city. On the cross, sacrificial blood flows down over His ears and thumbs and toes in a grizzly consecration ceremony, of sorts, for this Great High Priest. The last of His blood pools at the base of the cross as around an altar, confirming the death of the sacrifice and the reinstatement of mankind's fellowship with God.

This is the Lamb of God we serve. This is the source of bread and wine for our communion. This is the Great High Priest who carries our names on His breast, and these are our stripes laying open on His back. The Lamb has been judged instead of us, and we have gone free.

What is left but to offer Him praise and thanksgiving?

He shall see the labor of His soul, and be satisfied.
By His knowledge My righteous Servant shall
justify many, for He shall bear their iniquities
(Isaiah 53:11).

Prayer: Lord Jesus, were I to stop sinning from this day forward, were I to give my whole life in Your service, it would not be enough to earn a place for me in God's tent. You have done what I couldn't do. You have given what I never had to offer, just to make room for me at God's table. The height of my praise struggles to express the depth of my gratitude.

Deeper Still

Take your time in reading Isaiah 53.
Don't worry about finishing the entire chapter. Just read it slowly enough to register whether God wants you to pause over a verse and meditate on it. Stay with each verse as long as you need to, expressing your thanks as you do. Journal your thoughts.

Day 90

Home at Last

Before we begin read Leviticus 9:22–24

As soon as Moses, Aaron, and the other priests launch the tabernacle into its first day of ministry, God explodes from the Holy of Holies, burns the sacrifices, and fills the tent with smoke. It's Mount Sinai 2.0.

Almighty God is making a joyful shout and no one's moving until He's done with it. What triggers God's happy dance isn't so much what just happened in the earthly tabernacle, but what it foreshadows. He knows the one against whom He modeled every part and form and function of the tent is on His way. Christ will not only *be* the dwelling place in which God lives with His family, He will *fill* it with children—making them into tabernacles fit to accommodate the Father, Son, and Holy Spirit.

Everywhere we've looked in the tabernacle, we've seen evidence of God's unquenchable desire to have us dwell with Him. Wood wrapped in gold, linen laced with gold, ordinary humans decorated in glory—all speak of a God who wants to touch and protect and beautify us.

Though the main character in the story told by the tabernacle designs is Jesus, we are woven through and through. The Lord apparently loves us so much, He can hardly refrain from giving us leading roles alongside

Him. Where we don't measure up, He plays our stand-in. His righteousness, acceptance, perfect peace, Godly wisdom, and whole-hearted devotion all become ours at the altar.

Throughout the journey, Jesus has been, and will continue to be, our guide in the chaos of the courtyard, in the quiet of the holy place, and before the face of God in the Holy of Holies. Our names are remembered, pronounced, and written in even the deepest places in the tabernacle, marking us as permanent fixtures in His dwelling place.

Before I found a home in God's tent, my heart had an empty hole that only He could fill. I'm convinced God's heart too has empty places that won't be filled by anyone but us. What would the tabernacle be, after all, if its sockets fell short a half shekel? How would the walls in the holy place stand if any of them lacked a board? Which part of the tent would be exposed to the elements if the goat hair curtains were missing a single panel?

He is a God of full measures and He's longing for you to take your place in His tent. He won't stop searching or weaving or building until He determines every stitch, every piece, every stone, every scrap of linen is present and accounted for. We are that stitch, that piece, that stone. He will miss you if you aren't there. And so, for that matter, will the rest of us in His family.

Before you were a gleam in your mother's eye, God was preparing a place for you. He has swept aside everything that might hinder your way into the deepest, chambers of His heart.

Dive through His tent flap and let Him hide you in His shelter. You are His long-awaited, heart's desire.

*Then the LORD will create above every dwelling place of Mount
Zion, and above her assemblies, a cloud and smoke by day and
the shining of a flaming fire by night. For over all the glory
there will be a covering. And there will be a tabernacle for shade
in the daytime from the heat, for a place of refuge, and for a
shelter from storm and rain
(Isaiah 4:5–6).*

Prayer: One thing I have desired of you Lord, that will I
seek: that I may dwell in Your house all the days of my
life, to behold Your beauty, and to inquire in Your courts.
Hide me in Your secret place and I will offer sacrifices of
joy in Your tabernacle.

Deeper Still

Read Psalm 27:4–6 (from which this prayer was adapted).
We are His dwelling place and He is ours. Take a
moment to journal your gratitude to the Lord for making
a permanent place for you within the curtains of His
tabernacle.

Week Six

Discussion Questions

This week we talked about the need for two different fires to burn the sacrifices, and the difference between sin and trespass offerings. We learned the order in which the offerings were placed on the altar and God's response to their presentation. Choose one or more of the following questions to consider on your own or discuss as a group.

1. What do you think it was like for Jesus to experience total separation from God on the cross? What's the difference between experiencing seasons when God seems far away and the possibility of permanent separation from Him?

2. Think of a time you initially refused to do something God's way, then repented and corrected your behavior. What did that trespass cost you or your loved ones? What did it cost God to have you stray? Take some time to thank Jesus for making restitution for every one of your failures.

3. Why do you think God wants us to take care of our responsibilities to make restitution before we come to Him for forgiveness?

4. Talk about Jesus as the sin, burnt, grain, drink, trespass, and peace offerings. For which of these sacrifices are you most grateful to have Jesus as your substitute on the altar and why?

5. Questions? Insights? Look for "A Place for Me in God's Tent" on Facebook and join the conversation.

Postscript

This devotional must end somewhere, so here is where we'll stop. We certainly haven't covered every detail in the tabernacle, but should we unwrap the whole of it, "I suppose that even the world itself could not contain the books that would be written" (John 21:25). This book isn't meant to be an exhaustive study but a conversation starter.

As you read on in the Scriptures, continue to look for more references to the tabernacle and its symbolism. What else might we glean from all the detail God's left us in its design? Discuss the possibilities with your friends to see what these things might mean.

One day, the tabernacle gives way to a temple made of stones. Rebuilt more than once, even the temple will prove impermanent as a dwelling place for God. All along, He's seeking human hearts for His ultimate home.

As He pursues a place in our hearts, He opens His own heart to make a place for us. John 1:14 talks about the Word becoming flesh and dwelling among us. In the Greek, however, the wording is more like He became flesh and spread His tabernacle over us. Just as we are His dwelling place, He is ours. Truly, "we abide in Him, and He in us" (1 John 4:13).

Wherever we go, the tabernacle abides within and about us. God's fire, power, wisdom, nourishment, and guidance fill and surround us more genuinely and substantially than their symbolic counterparts did the Old Testament tent.

If life still feels like a wilderness, remember you travel *as* a tabernacle, *in* a tabernacle. The bronze altar of the cross is perpetually aflame for you with forgiveness, acceptance, and peace. The smoke of the incense altar never stops rising on your behalf, never quits ascending with your prayers for others. The light of His lamp burns brightly within, giving you access to the mind of Christ. The bread and wine of His spiritual nourishment is always on His table, ready to satisfy you with life and joy. And the presence of God fills and surrounds you like a cloud of smoke during the day and a pillar of fire at night.

Our Great High Priest has spread the fabric of His tent over us and transformed us into His own special tabernacles. How can we not be at peace?

There's a place for you in God's tabernacle, and in God's tabernacle, there's a place for me.

Works Cited

Brand, C., C. Draper , A. England, S. Bond, E. Clendenen. T. C. Butler (Eds.). 2003. Almond. In *Holman Illustrated Bible Dictionary*. Nashville, TN: Holman Bible Publishers.

Conner, Kevin J. 1976. *The Tabernacle of Moses*. Portland, OR: City Christian Publishing.

DeHaan, M. R., M.D. 1955. *The Tabernacle*. Grand Rapids, MI: Zondervan Publishing House.

Dickens, Charles. 1911. *A Christmas Carol*. London: Hodder and Stoughton.

Dyer, C. H. (1985). Jeremiah. In J. F. Walvoord & R. B. Zuck (Eds.), *The Bible Knowledge Commentary: An Exposition of the Scriptures*. Wheaton, IL: Victor Books.

Edersheim, Alfred. 1994. *The Temple: Its Ministry and Services*. Peabody, MA: Hendrickson Publishers Marketing, LLC.

Epp, Theodore. 1976. *Portraits of Christ in the Tabernacle*. Lincoln, NB: Good News Broadcasting Association.

Hyde, Daniel R. 2012. *God in Our Midst: The Tabernacle and Our Relationship with God*. Ann Arbor, MI: Reformation Trust Publishing.

Jamieson, R., A. R. Fausset, and D. Brown. 1997. *Commentary Critical and Explanatory on the Whole Bible*. Vol. 1. Oak Harbor, WA: Logos Research Systems, Inc.

Jukes, Andrew. 1966. *The Law of the Offerings*. Grand Rapids: Kregel Publications.

Levy, David M. 2003. *The Tabernacle: Shadows of the Messiah*. Grand Rapids, MI: Kregel Publications.

Soltau, Henry W. 1971. *The Holy Vessels and Furniture of the Tabernacle*. Grand Rapids, MI: Kregel Publications.

—. 1972. *The Tabernacle, the Priesthood, and the Offerings* . Grand Rapids: Kregel Publications.

Stern, David H. 1995. *Jewish New Testament Commentary*. Clarksville, MD: Jewish New Testament Publications.

Strong, James. 1987. *The Tabernacle of Israel: Its Structure and Symbolism*. Grand Rapids, MI : Kregel Publications.

Thomas, R. L. 1998. *New American Standard Hebrew-Aramaic and Greek Dictionaries : updated edition*. Anaheim: Foundation Publications, Inc.

Whitfield, Frederick. 1884. *The Tabernacle Priesthood and Offerings of Israel*. London: James Nisbet & Company.

63494529R00217